How to

ELIMINATE DISCRIMINATORY PRACTICES

A guide to

EEO COMPLIANCE

How to

ELIMINATE DISCRIMINATORY PRACTICES

A guide to

EEO COMPLIANCE

The staff of HUMANIC DESIGNS DIVISION
of INFORMATION SCIENCE INCORPORATED

amacom A DIVISION OF AMERICAN MANAGEMENT ASSOCIATIONS

Library of Congress Cataloging in Publication Data

Information Science Incorporated. Humanic Designs
    Division.
    How to eliminate discriminatory practices.

    Bibliography: p.
    1. Discrimination in employment—United States—
Handbooks, manuals, etc. I. Title.
HD4903.5.U58I54 1975   658.1'2   75-2380
ISBN 0-8144-5396-1

First Printing

PREFACE

This publication is an outgrowth of a project supported by the U.S. Department of Labor, Manpower Administration, Office of Research and Development, and by the Equal Employment Opportunity Commission (EEOC), Washington, D.C. The initial work, begun in 1970, had the major objective of determining more effective ways of hiring and promoting minority group members and women in the private sector. In the early days of this demonstration project, Humanic Designs Division of Information Science Incorporated (formerly Humanic Designs Corporation) worked very closely with the staff of the EEOC's Office of Voluntary Programs and a variety of companies in order to develop a preliminary manual that would be useful in identifying systemic discrimination. The statistics and tables described in this text were subsequently developed by IScI into computer software for tracking and updating required data.

In the interactions related to these activities, HDD formalized the notion of *parity* and first experimented in its application. Furthermore, HDD helped to apply the notion of *systemic discrimination*. Many individuals and organizations, both private and public, were consulted in the process. The parceling out of credit for ideas is always difficult; in this instance, it is downright impossible. Indeed, this publication is truly the work of many, all of whom deserve credit.

It was the encouragement, ideas, and overall guidance of former EEOC chairman William Brown III that helped to make this book possible. Mr. Seymour Brandwein, Dr. Howard Rosen, and Ms. Juliet Brussel of the U.S. Department of Labor also played an important role in guiding us during those days. The principal investigators who were involved in the detailed analysis and testing were Dr. Oscar A. Ornati and Anthony F. Pisano. The technical direction was reinforced by Leonard Smith, Caroline Pezzullo, Neil Thompson, and Edward James. Many members of the Office of Voluntary Programs also contributed to these guidelines. I wish to thank Chris Roggerson, George Butler, and Jack Maddox of that office for their assistance. Finally, the typing and editing efforts of Irene Elber and Carol Paul made the book a reality.

How to Eliminate Discriminatory Practices is an updated summary of that work, cast into a mold helpful to managers in placing their organization in equal employment compliance. In addition, we have endeavored here to describe and clarify government guidelines and court decisions to make their spirit and their application more accessible to managers who are not themselves specialists in compliance or are unfamiliar with its specialized terminology. This publication thus is a recap of experience more than a definitive contribution to a still rapidly evolving field. Its continued applicability to the future compliance practice depends in part on the reader's keeping up to date on new regulations and court decisions.

In publishing this guide through AMACOM, we hope to launch a new level of awareness and practice that will help us all reach the goal of a society with truly nondiscriminatory employment practices.

Samuel B. Marks
President
Humanic Designs Division

FOREWORD

Most businessmen are well aware that the U.S. Equal Employment Opportunity Commission has the Congressional mandate to enforce Title VII of the Civil Rights Act of 1964. They also know that violations have been vigorously prosecuted. Most people, however, are surprised to learn that the Commission can also provide material assistance to employers who want to eliminate discrimination voluntarily. The concept of voluntary compliance has always been inherent to Title VII, although it has seldom been given serious consideration by industry.

Discrimination is usually thought to be the result of overt actions by prejudiced or biased individuals. While such discrimination in employment continues, fortunately it is declining. But the fact is that most discrimination is a result of policies, procedures, and employment systems which, however inadvertently or neutrally applied, affect some people differently from others. When they are applied to the detriment of the protected classes, there is systemic discrimination. It is insidious, usually unintentional, and its detection requires careful search and analysis by the organization.

That is what this publication is all about—systemic discrimination and an organization's obligation to analyze the total employment processes, detect systemic discrimination, eliminate it, and make the affected party or parties whole. Employers who are seriously committed to eliminating discrimination in all forms and in changing concentrations of minorities and women in lower-paying job categories (particularly in those industries noted for providing low average earnings) can save themselves time, anguish, and money through voluntary analysis and corrective action. Substantive positive change will not come about if companies simply continue to play the "numbers game."

William H. Brown, III
Chairman
Equal Employment Opportunity Commission
(1969 to 1973)

CONTENTS

INTRODUCTION

As every employer should know by now, powerful federal legislation proscribing discrimination in employment has been in effect since 1964. While antidiscrimination legislation has existed since the Civil War, no prior law has had the impact of the Civil Rights Act of 1964. Very simply, Title VII of that act prohibits discrimination in all aspects of employment on the basis of race, color, religion, sex, or national origin.

Title VII of the Civil Rights Act is enforced by the Equal Employment Opportunity Commission (EEOC). EEOC's mission is to investigate charges of discriminatory practice and to prosecute, if necessary, violations of Title VII. The Commission also has the authority to initiate investigations and, if necessary, charges of discriminatory practice, and many dramatic and expensive settlements have resulted from the exercise of this power.

On the heels of the Civil Rights Act, President Lyndon B. Johnson signed Executive Order 11246 (and later 11375) which prohibits discrimination in employment by federal contractors or subcontractors on essentially the same five bases and created another enforcement agency, the Office of Federal Contract Compliance (OFCC). The OFCC, in turn, designated compliance agencies within 13 other federal government agencies and bodies (among them, for example, the Department of Treasury, Atomic Energy Commission, the Departments of Defense, Agriculture, and Health, Education, and Welfare), giving each jurisdiction over appropriate industries.

Over time, the OFCC issued a series of administrative orders. The most important of them are now generally referred to as the "Revised Orders." Employers are primarily concerned with Revised Orders No. 4 and No. 14. These orders not only proscribe discrimination; they require the employer to analyze his employment process, identify deficiencies, and take corrective action. All these activities are subject to periodic scrutiny by the appropriate compliance agency. If an employer is found to be noncompliant, the penalty may be the loss of the government contract (or license) enjoyed by the contractor.

This manual is not intended as a primer for neophytes. Although the reader is probably already familiar with such things as individual charges and class action suits, a brief review of the full meaning of the federal laws and reporting requirements is in order. To assist the reader, a list of definitions of terms in the special vocabulary of antidiscrimination legislation and enforcement is included at the back of this book. Since these terms are used often, and always within their special frame of reference, the reader is urged to study the definitions before reading further.

TITLE VII OF THE CIVIL RIGHTS ACT OF 1964

To the surprise of many, Title VII says nothing about numbers, goals, and timetables. To put it in somewhat oversimplified terms, Title VII merely says that discrimination in employment on the bases of race, color, religion, sex, or national origin is illegal and that violations can be prosecuted and corrected under law.

What is not well understood is that "employment" means more than recruitment, application, and hiring. Under Title VII, employment includes compensation, promotion, termination, benefits, work assignment, career progression, shift assignment, and virtually any company activity which affects the status, income, advancement, or work environment of any individual employee or class of employees. Discriminatory practice, *intentional* or *inadvertent,* must be eliminated from each of these aspects of the employment process. Under Title VII, it is the employer's *implicit* obligation to discover discriminatory practice and eliminate it. The employer is also implicitly obliged to "make whole" all persons who have been denied equal employment opportunity. This may require promotion (when openings permit), back pay, special training programs, or other corrective actions.

THE EXECUTIVE ORDERS AND THE REVISED ORDERS

What is implicit in Title VII is explicit in Revised Order No. 4. The employer who is a federal contractor or licensee is explicitly instructed to conduct a *utilization analysis* and write an "Affirmative Action Plan" explaining how he will (a) correct any deficiencies discovered in the process of utilization analysis, and (b) attain a compliant posture. This, of course, will include the specification of actions intended to make aggrieved parties, or "affected classes," whole.

Utilization analysis requires the employer to:

— determine by race, sex, and sex-within-race the current work force distribution (vertically and horizontally, for all units and subunits of the organization) of minorities and women in the organization.
— compare his employment of minorities and women with their availability in the external labor market (or markets).
— determine, through the above comparisons, where his employment (again, across all units and subunits of organization) is not statistically consonant with the incidence of minorities and women (who possess the requisite skills for various types and levels of jobs) in the labor market.
— establish Affirmative Action Plan (AAP) goals and timetables to attract and employ minorities and women with the requisite skills at a rate compatible with the rate at which job openings or opportunities will occur within the organization (through expansion or turnover).
— conduct an analysis of the applicant flow process, recruitment effort, placement process, promotion process (job to job, pay grade to pay grade, etc.), compensation process, and termination process (voluntary and involuntary) to determine whether the protected classes participate equitably in these processes. (These analyses depend upon historical data. Revised Order No. 4 requires federal contractors to retain at least six months' history on each of these aspects of the employment process.)
— where statistical disparities are found, investigate to determine whether they are discriminatory; if so, include in the AAP the steps intended to eliminate the practice and to relieve ("make whole") the affected persons or classes.

In summary, Revised Order No. 4 tells the employer to: determine where he is in his current utilization of the protected classes; determine where he should be, through comparison with the appropriate external labor market(s) and analysis of his employment process, and determine how he intends to go from where he is to where he should be by creating an AAP.

TITLE VII, REVISED ORDER NO. 4, AND SYSTEMIC DISCRIMINATION

Although established under different authority and enforced by different agencies (with respectively different powers of enforcement), both Title VII and Revised Order No. 4 tell the employer that he must not discriminate in employment and that *he* must determine whether he is doing so, intentionally or otherwise. Self-analysis is therefore the key to compliance. This manual is a guide to effective self-analysis for the purpose of discovering and correcting discrimination in employment. But before the reader is ready for self-analysis (or self-audit), he must understand the concept of *systemic discrimination,* the form of discrimination which has been at the heart of most (if not all) major EEOC-instigated conciliations and court-adjudicated settlements.

Discrimination occurs in two forms. Obviously discrimination exists when the personal biases of an individual in authority enter the decision-making process in employment matters to the detriment of applicants or employees. Discrimination also occurs, however, in much more insidious form. It is harder to detect, is usually unintentional and inadvertent, and almost invariably results from policies, practices, selection criteria, and decision-making criteria which affect the protected classes differently (again to their detriment) from Caucasian applicants or employees. This is systemic discrimination. The now famous *Griggs v. Duke Power* case is the classic case in point and should be required reading for all managers. (See page 10.)

It is widely understood that employment tests (intelligence tests, skills tests, aptitude tests, and the like) are viewed as selection criteria and that they must be validated. It is *not* widely understood that such things as minimum educational levels, the questions asked during an interview, a stated requirement of the amount, or type, of prior work experience, performance evaluation systems, or anything that is used to measure, choose, select, decide among candidates, award a promotion or an increase, or terminate an employee, are also considered as selection criteria.

By definition, criteria are used to screen out the less-qualified and select the most- or best-qualified applicant. The Tower Amendment to Title VII guarantees the employer the right to use selection criteria at any step of the employment process, but the courts have continually insisted that all criteria must be neutrally applied and must be job-related. All such criteria (and tests), to paraphrase Chief Justice Burger's opinion in *Griggs v. Duke Power*, must measure the person for the job at hand and not just the person in the abstract. Thus it is not simply the employer's good intentions that will be measured. Well-intended or not, it is the *effect* of his policies, practices, and selection criteria that will be measured. If the effect of any criterion he employs is disparate, and if that disparity cannot be justified by a legitimate business necessity, it is in violation of the Act. The criterion must be re-evaluated in light of the job (or jobs) in question and, if the effects have been felt by an individual or group, those persons must be made whole.

As the Commission and the courts view it, discrimination on the basis of race, color, religion, sex, or national origin is discrimination against the *class* of people with the characteristic in common. Therefore, a statistical disparity at any step of the employment process (see Box 1 for an example) amply serves either agency as a prima facie indication of discriminatory practice.* Once such a statistical disparity comes to the attention of either the EEOC or the OFCC, the employer must prove, if he can, that the practice or criterion causing the disparity is not in violation. The employer has the obligation to conduct self-analyses to determine whether statistical disparities exist and whether they are the result of properly applied or job-related criteria. If statistical disparities are not the result of proper criteria, the employer must correct the practice and make whole the affected person.

This manual is intended to help employers locate such disparities and to ferret out systemic discrimination.

*The Tower Amendment makes clear that statistics alone do not constitute *proof*. The OFCC and the courts are consistent in their view that statistics can lead to an inference of discrimination sufficient to warrant further investigation, and that they can and will be used as evidence.

1

A unit bank has 100 incumbents in the position of Teller Trainee, 60 of whom are women.

Over the last six months, 50 people have been promoted to the next higher job of Teller. Thirty-five of the promotions went to men.

Although women participate in the relevant labor pool at the rate of 60 percent, they participate in the promotion process only at the rate of 30 percent. These figures lead to a presumption of discriminatory practice. The burden of proof to defend the issue is on the employer.

THE ORGANIZATION OF THE MANUAL

Part I of the manual covers some general considerations. The first section deals with systemic discrimination in depth, citing cases bearing upon its definition, and describes how systemic discrimination enters the personnel system and its subsystems. The second section deals with remedies; it describes typical results of a self-audit and indicates how an employer can go about developing remedial programs. It includes a brief description of what is needed in an Affirmative Action Plan and explains the EEOC Voluntary Compliance Agreement.

Part II presents the methodology for self-audit in great detail. It comprises seven units, or modules, which build successively one upon the other. The first two units provide instruction in the collection of data (but not the analysis of those data). The third unit deals with measurements of parity (comparisons of the internal distribution of the work force to the appropriate external labor market or markets). These measures provide the analyst with a broad, early means of determining whether there are presumptive indications of discrimination. Nothing presented in these first three units will establish whether a disparity legally constitutes a truly discriminatory practice. These issues are addressed in units five and six. Unit four identifies specific personnel practices, permits establishment of priorities for later work, and leads to the preliminary identification of other potential major compliance issues.

The fifth and sixth units outline the steps necessary to identify discrimination in recruitment, hiring, promotion, transfer, and termination. The work done in accordance with the first three sections is used at this point to determine whether or not systemic discrimination exists. Unit seven discusses the principles of the EEOC's "theory of relief" relative to the development of specific remedies and the setting of goals and timetables.

WHO CAN BEST USE THE MANUAL?

This book has been written for employers who sincerely wish to comply with the law and who need reliable means of determining whether they are or are not discriminating, intentionally or otherwise.

The great majority of personnel executives are unaware of the high cost of preparing, defending, conciliating, or losing a case on charges of individual discrimination. Many corporate personnel staffs persist in thinking that the law is directed against the "other fellow"—the smaller or less enlightened employer, the local union, or whatever. And many EEO coordinators see their major responsibility as finding "a good woman (or minority member) who is qualified for a promotion." The problems go far beyond such simplistic approaches.

Part I is directed principally to top management, because top management is prepared to look at traditional procedures with a more clinical and dispassionate eye than personnel staff people. Statements such as these come from top management:

"No company that I know of is in compliance. All we can do is work at it."

"In reviewing our promotion system, we have found that there really was no good reason for many of our practices."

Part II is technical and methodological. It is written primarily for the use of personnel staffs and line managers, and both ought to be fully aware of the major thrusts of the analytic process.

It should be kept in mind that this manual is only one of many documents to be used in bringing the employment system in compliance with equal employment requirements. The Equal Employment Opportunity Commission has published a series of documents to help employers in their efforts to comply with the law.* One such publication, *Equal Employment Opportunity and Affirmative Action: A Guidebook for Employers on Voluntary Programs*, presents the requirements of the law in clear, non-technical terms. The guidebook should be at hand when employers apply the techniques outlined in this volume. The procedures set forth have been applied successfully in a number of business situations and have been consistently effective in identifying those personnel procedures or practices which have a discriminatory effect on minorities and women.

*See Selected Readings in the back of this manual.

PART I

SYSTEMIC DISCRIMINATION

The policy of the United States government is to eliminate discrimination in *all* aspects of employment. Discrimination in employment is often traceable to a specific act of one individual as it bears upon another. It is the employer's continuing responsibility to present individual acts of discrimination and to correct the effects of such acts. But individual management or supervisory actions which result in discrimination may stem from the application of a general rule, policy, criterion, or personnel practice which is not discriminatory in intent.

The job-relatedness of hiring, placement, and promotion criteria, combined with the "business necessity" that led to their establishment, form the touchstone that measures discrimination. Whether a practice, policy, or criterion that is applied across the board has in fact a discriminatory impact upon minorities and women is tested against job-relatedness. If it is not job-related, then it is discriminatory. The issue of job-related selection criteria is at the core of the problem, as established by the courts in case after case. *Griggs v. Duke Power* remains the watershed case in the court history of the jurisprudence. (Box 2 contains a summary of that decision.)

Without yielding in its legal obligation to defend separate individuals who are discriminated against, the EEOC's position is that in order to fulfill its congressional mandate, it must have the employer's cooperation in rectifying and/or avoiding practices that have a discriminatory, disparate effect on

2

Highlights of the Griggs v. Duke Power Co. Decision

"The objective of Congress in the enactment of Title VII is plain from the language of the statute. It was to achieve equality of employment opportunities and remove barriers that have operated in the past to favor an identifiable group of white employees. Under the Act, practices, procedures, or tests neutral on their face, and even neutral in terms of intent, cannot be maintained if they operate to 'freeze' the status quo of prior discriminatory employment practices."

*　　　*　　　*

". . . Congress did not intend by Title VII, however, to guarantee a job to every person regardless of qualifications. In short, the Act does not command that any person be hired simply because he was formerly the subject of discrimination, or because he is a member of a minority group. Discriminatory preference for any group, minority or majority, is precisely and only what Congress has proscribed. What is required by Congress is the removal of artificial, arbitrary, and unnecessary barriers to employment when the barriers operate invidiously to discriminate on the basis of racial or other impermissible classification.

". . . The Act proscribes not only overt discrimination but also practices that are fair in form, but discriminatory in operation. The touchstone is business necessity. If an employment practice which operates to exclude Negroes cannot be shown to be related to job performance, the practice is prohibited.

"On the record before us, neither the high school completion requirement nor the general intelligence test is shown to bear a demonstrable relationship to successful performance of the jobs for which it was used. Both were adopted, as the Court of Appeals noted, without meaningful study of their relationship to job-performance ability. Rather, a vice president of the Company testified, the requirements were instituted on the Company's judgment that they generally would improve the overall quality of the work force.

"The evidence, however, shows that employees who have not completed high school or taken the tests have continued to perform satisfactorily and make progress in departments for which the high school and test criteria are now used. The promotion record of present employees who would not be able to meet the new criteria thus suggests the possibility that the requirements may not be needed even for the limited purpose of preserving the avowed policy of advancement within the Company. In the context of this case, it is unnecessary to

2 (continued)

reach the question whether testing requirements that take into account capability for the next succeeding position or related future promotion might be utilized upon a showing that such long range requirements fulfill a genuine business need. In the present case the Company has made no such showing.

"... We do not suggest that either the District Court or the Court of Appeals erred in examining the employer's intent; but good intent or absence of discriminatory intent does not redeem employment procedures or testing mechanisms that operate as 'built-in headwinds' for minority groups and are unrelated to measuring job capability.

"The Company's lack of discriminatory intent is suggested by special efforts to help the under-educated employees through Company financing of two-thirds the cost of tuition for high school training. But Congress directed the thrust of the Act to the *consequences* of employment practices, not simply the motivation. More than that, Congress has placed on the employer the burden of showing that any given requirement must have a manifest relationship to the employment in question."

*   *   *

"Nothing in the Act precludes the use of testing or measuring procedures; obviously they are useful. What Congress has forbidden is giving these devices and mechanisms controlling force unless they are demonstrably a reasonable measure of job performance. Congress has not commanded that the less qualified be preferred over the better qualified simply because of minority origins. Far from disparaging job qualifications as such, Congress has made such qualifications the controlling factor, so that race, religion, nationality, and sex become irrelevant. What Congress has commanded is that any tests used must measure the person for the job and not the person in the abstract."

Excerpts from the decision of the Supreme Court of the United States, *Griggs vs. Duke Power Co.*, 401 U.S. 424 (1971).

minority groups or women as a class. (A disparate effect is one in which the proportion of members affected in one group is statistically different from the proportion of members affected in another group.) Such discrimination is called systemic.

This section cites EEOC documents and court cases that define systemic discrimination. (See Box 3.) It also describes the many ways in which normal and even apparently efficient personnel systems tend to incorporate misunderstandings of business need which may transform the personnel systems into vehicles of discrimination.

3

Title VII discrimination is more than discrimination against one individual......

Racial discrimination is, by definition, class discrimination and to require a multiplicity of separate, identical charges before the EEOC, filed against the same employer, as a prerequisite to relief through resort to the court would tend to frustrate our system of justice and order....

> Excerpt from the decision of the U.S. Court of Appeals, Fifth Circuit (New Orleans), *Oatis v. Crown Zellerbach Corporation*, 398 F. 2d 496 (1968).

At issue is the question whether the offer and acceptance of a promotion, subsequent to the filing of a class action alleging systemic racial discrimination renders the suit moot as to the employee individually or to the class he represents. We hold that the action is not moot on either score....

The problem arises from the unique structure of Title VII which limits access to the courts by conditioning the filing of a suit upon a previous administrative charge with the EEOC whose function is to effectuate the Act's policy of voluntary conference, persuasion and conciliation as the principal tools of enforcement....

Although there are restrictions both in time and pre-conditions for court action this does not minimize the role of ostensibly private litigation in effectuating the congressional policies. To the contrary, this magnifies its importance while at the same time utilizing the powerful catalyst of conciliation through EEOC. The suit is therefore more than a private claim by the employee seeking the particular job which is at the bottom of the charge of unlawful discrimination filed with EEOC. When conciliation has failed—either outright or by reason of the expiration of the statutory time-table—that individual, often obscure, takes on the mantle of the sovereign.... And the charge itself is something more than the single claim that a particular job has been denied him. Rather, it is a dual one: (1) a specific job, promotion, etc. has actually been denied and (2) this was due to Title VII forbidden discrimination....

Whether in name or not, the suit is perforce a sort of class action for fellow employees similarly situated. Consequently, while we do not here hold that such a "private Attorney General" is powerless absent court approval to dismiss his suit ... the court, over the suitor's protest, may not do it for him without ever judicially resolving ... the controversial issue of employer unlawful discrimination....

> Excerpts from the decision of the U.S. Court of Appeals, Fifth Circuit (New Orleans), *Jenkins v. United Gas Corporation*, 400 F. 2d 28 (1968).

SYSTEMIC DISCRIMINATION DEFINED

The EEOC's definition of systemic discrimination, derived from court decisions, is incorporated in the handbook *Proving Discrimination,* prepared by the Office of Compliance, Investigation Division (August 1971, as amplified), from which the pertinent passages are cited here:

Discrimination is caused in two ways. *The more important of these is known as systemic discrimination.* This means that the denial of equal opportunity is the inevitable consequence of some business practice, and does not involve or require any specific action against the discriminatee.

... The hallmark of systemic discrimination is that it involves the use of apparently neutral criteria, which are in most cases applied to all classes alike (in some cases the system is both inherently discriminatory and discriminatorily administered), which results in the denial of equal opportunity. The identification of these apparently neutral criteria is the touchstone of an investigation of a case involving systemic discrimination.

Every employer, regardless of size or the nature of goods and services produced, maintains personnel practices and procedures in order to manage and control the employment process. An assessment of personnel policies and practices will reveal those practices which create a disparate effect. Such analysis constitutes the first essential step in achieving consonance with the requirements of the law.

Finding procedures that have a disparate effect is not in itself sufficient identification of discrimination; it only forces the next question: Are the procedures "necessary to the safe and efficient operation of the business"? In many cases litigated so far, the claim of business necessity has been found by the court to be invalid; yet there may be situations in which such procedures can be shown to constitute a business necessity. (See Box 4 for such a case.)

Few of the managers surveyed in the course of developing this manual understood that disparate effect signaled the presence of systemic discrimination, and fewer understood that this did not necessarily mean that an illegal act had been committed. Furthermore, even fewer knew how to cope with a situation of disparate effect.

The Conference Board report entitled *Non-Discrimination in Employment* cites one employer's change of perspective on Title VII that parallels many statements of employers in our survey:

I had first assumed that the validation studies talked about in the EEOC Guidelines on Employee Selection Procedures would be required for all our employee selection standards and practices. Suddenly I noticed that this was not the case. It was only those tests and procedures that had an adverse impact on the employment opportunities of protected groups that needed to be validated.

If we dropped all discriminatory standards and changed all our procedures so that approximately the same proportion of all groups were proceeding through each step of our staffing procedures, there would be no adverse impact on any protected group and we would not be required to conduct any validation studies at all. We would not be discriminating against any protected group, so the Guidelines would never be triggered.

They would come into play only when we felt it was important, as a matter of business necessity, to use a discriminatory standard or procedure. What the Guidelines spelled out was exactly how we needed to go about establishing the relationship of a discriminatory standard or procedure to job performance.

Naturally we were also expected to have made a good faith search for a less discriminatory way to achieve the same job performance. We couldn't very well, for example, insist on an electrical engineering degree if we know that all the technical knowledge needed for the particular job could be taught in a three-week training course. Too few minority group members and women had electrical degrees. It would make far better sense for us to provide the three weeks of job-specific training.

DISCRIMINATION IN THE PERSONNEL SYSTEM

In order to understand the pervasiveness of systemic discrimination, it seems most useful to describe the decisions and actions taken right from the start in setting up a personnel system. This section focuses on the points at which discrimination can occur and can lead to disparate effect by tracing the personnel placement function in the context of the total system. This counterposing of the component parts of the personnel process and bias is useful because the process described in the audit is similar. Indeed, the audit tests the totality of the personnel system to uncover where the biases in personnel rules make for disparate effects.

4

Discriminatory, but necessary, employment standards.

From the evidence, the trial court found an absence of an intent to discriminate on the part of United in hiring its flight officers. While it is important to examine the intent of a company charged with discriminatory effect, Title VII is aimed at the consequences of employment practices, not simply the motivation. . . . Thus, when a plaintiff is claiming that the criteria used by a company in screening job applicants discriminate against a minority group, he needs only establish that the use of such criteria has a discriminatory result. . . . It is not necessary to prove a discriminatory intent but only that the discriminatory criteria were used deliberately, not accidentally.

In order to establish that United's flight officer qualifications resulted in discrimination against blacks, the appellant showed that out of the approximately 5900 flight officers in United's employ at the time of the trial, only nine were blacks. Appellant contends that these statistics establish a prima facie case of racial discrimination. United claims that these bare statistics establish nothing unless accompanied by similar information as to the number of qualified black applicants for the flight officer position. The circuitousness of this bootstrap argument becomes obvious when one recalls that it is United's qualifications for flight officer that appellant claims are discriminatory against blacks. We hold, therefore, that by showing the minuscule number of black flight officers in United's employ, the appellant established a prima facie case of racial discrimination in hiring practices.

4 (continued)

Employment practices which are inherently discriminatory may nevertheless be valid if a business necessity can be shown. And pre-employment qualifications which result in discrimination may be valid if they are shown to be job-related. Thus, once the appellant had established a prima facie case of racial discrimination, the burden fell upon United to show that its qualifications for flight officers were job-related. We agree.

The two job qualifications that appellant challenges are the requirements of a college degree and a minimum of 500 flight hours. The evidence at trial showed that United does not train applicants to be pilots but instead requires that their applicants be pilots at the time of their application. It cannot seriously be contended that such a requirement is not job-related. United also showed, through the use of statistics, that applicants who have higher flight hours are more likely to succeed in the rigorous training program which United flight officers go through after they are hired. The statistics clearly showed that 500 hours was a reasonable minimum to require of applicants to insure their ability to pass United's training program. The evidence also showed that because of the high cost of the training program, it is important to United that those who begin the training program eventually become flight officers. This is an example of business necessity. We conclude that the evidence amply supports a finding that the requirement of 500 hours flight time is job-related.

With regard to the college degree requirement, United officials testified that it was a requirement which could be waived if the applicant's other qualifications were superior especially if he had a lot [of] ... flight time in high speed jet aircraft. The evidence shows that United flight officers go through a rigorous training course upon being hired and then are required to attend intensive refresher courses at six-month intervals. ... United officials testified that the possession of a college degree indicated that the applicant had the ability to understand and retain concepts and information given in the atmosphere of a classroom or training program. Thus, a person with a college degree, particularly one in the "hard" sciences, is more able to cope with the initial training program and the unending series of refresher courses. ... In reviewing the trial court's findings on this matter, we are limited to the clearly erroneous standard. ... We conclude that the evidence supports the trial court's findings that United's requirements are job-related.

When a job requires a small amount of skill and training and the consequences of hiring an unqualified applicant are insignificant, the courts should examine closely any pre-employment standard or criteria which discriminate against minorities. In such a case, the employer should have a heavy burden to demonstrate to the court's satisfaction that his employment criteria are job-related. On the other hand, when the job clearly requires a high degree of skill and the economic and human risks involved in hiring an unqualified applicant are great, the employer bears a correspondingly lighter burden to show that his employment criteria are job-related. ... The job of airline flight officer is clearly such a job. United's flight officers pilot aircraft worth as much as $20 million and transport as many as 300 passengers per flight. The risks involved in hiring an unqualified applicant are staggering. The public interest clearly lies in having the most highly qualified persons available to pilot airliners. The courts, therefore, should proceed with great caution before requiring an employer to lower his pre-employment standards for such a job. We conclude that United Airlines met its burden of proving that its employment requirements are job-related and that the trial court's finding in that regard is not clearly erroneous.

Excerpts from the decision of the U.S. Court of Appeals, Tenth Circuit (Denver), *Spurlock v. United Airlines*, F. 2d, 5FEP Cases 17.

The approach used here, to the end of this section, is derived from *The Employment Process as a System* by the California Fair Employment Practices Commission (Special Studies Subcommittee, Technical Advisory Committee on Testing). The quoted material is derived from the California FEPC study; the annotations that follow represent our understanding of the court's and the EEOC's positions.

1. Organizational Needs and Goals

"It involves the determination and identification of new products or services or a modification of products or services that are to be produced or performed ... the organization identifies potential and target markets ... evaluates the financial returns to be expected, examines the relationship of the new product or service to existing business activities, and performs other related activities. ... "

Comment: Rarely does this step in itself lead to the introduction of employment biases.

2. Resources Needed

"This step is an examination of all of the resources required to produce or to provide the product or service identified in Step 1. At this preliminary stage, no steps are taken to obtain any resources, facilities, equipment and manpower or to determine if or where or how they can be obtained. ... It is after this step that the different systems will diverge—the financial requirement system to provide the finances necessary, the facilities system to provide adequate space, the employment system to acquire the necessary manpower."

Comment: This step involves primarily the identification of what is needed. Again, rarely does bias enter into the picture here. On the other hand, certain invalid social presumptions about manpower needs may surface. Thus if a business is launching a new feeder airline, the presumption that stewardesses are needed would be invalid.

3. Identification of Work to Be Performed

"This step involves the following activities: defining the steps necessary to produce or provide the product or services; determining the sequence in which the steps are to be performed; specifying the intermediate outputs occurring; identifying the amount and kinds of *knowledge and skill requirements at each of these steps;* and determining the groupings of work that will be combined to form jobs or job groupings. ... For the purpose of the employment process, it is important to note that decisions are made in employment which will determine the activities to be performed, and therefore the skills, knowledge, etc. to be provided by the workers. ... "

Comment: The identification of the work to be performed involves many interactions with planners dealing with equipment, and the process permits little bias. On the other hand, prevention of future disparate effect enters in here when the knowledge and skill requirements for employees carrying out certain operations are misstated. For the major jobs, a useful way to avoid setting improper skill and knowledge requirements is by careful analysis of each position's technical requirement. This involves the development of precise job descriptions and job evaluation. To be truly nondiscriminatory, the job evaluations need to be translated in terms of skill and knowledge requirements. There are a variety of ways in which this can be done. One of them is to carry out job task and requirements analyses (JTRAs*) which ensure that the skill and/or knowledge required of employees is truly job-related.

4. The Surveying of the Labor Market

"This step involves a survey of the available and/or obtainable labor skills. The survey conducted may be a sophisticated one involving an examination of such factors as: regional facilities; rate of growth or decline of the local labor force; an examination of the degree of skill; the stability of work, and the wage level paid by other employers in the same labor market; and the level and skill of the presently unemployed. Or, it may be limited to one manager calling another manager who is a friend or acquaintance. Regardless of the sophistication of the survey, it should be noted that the information obtained is one factor affecting later decisions with regard to (1) the allocation of activities to jobs; (2) advertising strategy; (3) training, etc."

Comment: Bias can enter at this step if assumptions are incorrect as to the skills, attitudes, and motivation of certain portions of the labor market. One example has to do with the assumptions made about the trainability, motivation, and willingness of persons designated "unemployable" just a few years ago. If the source of the information on which the assumptions are based is biased, or if the information gathered by the source is incorrect, merely altering procedures and methods can mean that significant numbers of this group will be utilized. If minority group members or persons with limited education or with language or cultural difficulties are removed from consideration because of such false assumptions, the design of further steps of the employment process will reflect this and may be inappropriate for those groups. It may lead to disparate applicant flows and insufficient minority outreach.

5. Identification of Specific Jobs

"Here the decisions are made on how to group activities into jobs. The following types of questions are answered: Which activities can be done by the same person? How many different activities can one person perform? What level of complexity is involved in each? Considerations that enter at this point include expected wage levels appropriate for different groupings of skills, the number of people required in a 'crew,' etc."

*Developed by Humanic Designs Division of Information Science Inc.

Comment: Inertia is a barrier to optimal utilization of persons here: the failure to reexamine well-developed ideas concerning the way in which skills and tools are grouped into jobs and occupations. Also important here in avoiding disparate effects is the building of rational career ladders. Indeed, unless the sequence of jobs is structured so as to assure that in each job the worker learns more elements of the next job, one builds in either disparate effects or dead-end jobs. The presence of either may be interpreted as representing discriminatory practices.

6. Development of Job Descriptions

"The job description is used by personnel in employment, wage and salary, and labor relations areas to understand the job content and activities and to deal with applicants for, and incumbents of, the job. The job description normally contains the following information: the tasks to be performed, the physical and environmental demands, communications required of the incumbent, his location in the organizational structure, and any special requirements needed for the job such as licenses, certifications, or training either before or after employment."

Comment: Many a job description fails to state the general skill and knowledge requirements of the bulk of the job, and vague assumptions about them are applied instead. It is usually here that a high school diploma is inserted into the requirements. When such a requirement is not job-related it is discriminatory.

7. Development of Selection Criteria

"The next step is to translate the job description into requirements to be established for applicants. This involves the determination of the degree to which skills, interests, experiences, education, personality characteristics and physical characteristics are required for, and/or related to, performing the activities of the job. This translation of job description to employment requirements is, of course, one of the crucial and most difficult sets of judgments to make. Inappropriate requirements may introduce selection bias by rejecting a larger proportion of some applicant groups than others."

Comment: The process of evaluating whether the selection criteria established in this step are in fact related to job performance is termed *validation.* Validating selection requirements is related to employee performance. At the same time, it can reveal whether bias is present in the requirements. The level at which such requirements are established is also a significant factor. Requirements can be established at levels that reject or accept the great majority of applicants.

8. Development of a Selection Plan

"After the criteria are established, a plan is developed for examining the qualifications of applicants. This plan includes the determination of how to measure the factors desired (application blank, reference check, physical examination, psychological test, interview, etc.); who will conduct the measurement; who will interpret it; the order in which the measures will be taken; which measures will be taken; which measures will be hurdles; which must be passed and which will be evaluated in combination with others; what weighing of factors will be done; who will make the final employment decision; and who will inform the applicant of the decision."

Comment: Selection bias can enter at this step when the method of measurement systematically favors one group over another. For example, if the instructions for taking a psychological test, or for completing an application form, are couched in language that is easily understood by college graduates but not by applicants with eighth-grade education, the procedure is biased in favor of those with more education. This is inappropriate unless that education is specifically required for effective job performance.

Bias is also present to the degree that the plan makes it easier for one group of applicants to present their most favorable attributes. Subtle cultural differences play a role here; for example, knowing when and to whom to provide information and knowing what kinds of information will assist one's case is critical when an interviewer combines the total package of measures and makes the final decision. *The selection plan should explain to the applicant what information is desired at each step, and each applicant should be encouraged to volunteer helpful information.* This is particularly important in avoiding disparate placement of women.

9. Identification of Expected Applicants and Sources

"The organization develops an 'expected target' applicant for the available openings, mostly from their past experience with similar people. Some aspects of the picture of the 'expected target' include where he lives, where he works, what media he uses for information, what he wants from a job, his attitude toward employment, and how and when he will contact the employer. All of these are required for determining the activities to be conducted in order to acquire a supply of applicants."

Comment: If an employer fails to include one segment of the potential applicant population in his target, he is not likely to have many applicants from that segment. The resultant limited applicant flow is not necessarily discriminatory, yet the effect is identical, screening members of that segment from available jobs. Recognition of such overlooked targets can be remedied by advertising in minority newspapers, setting up employment offices in minority areas, and establishing transportation facilities.

10. Initial Contacts—Pre-employment Interview/Assessment

"The impressions and attitudes that develop as a result of this event are quite pervasive; they frequently determine the way in which each of the parties communicates to the other. The applicant generally makes the initial contact. He contacts the employer by mail, telephone, or in person. The physical and social conditions that prevail at the time of this initial 'set' toward the employer, and the applicant's attitude, appearance, and response to the conditions that exist determine the employer's response to the applicant. The applicant generally provides an indication of interest in employment, and possibly interest in a specific opening or line of work. The employer's representative responds by presenting information or requiring information from the applicant, either in written or oral form. The representative also decides what step the applicant takes next: whether to enter him into the funnel of the evaluation process."

Comment: Treating minorities differently at this point is common. The personnel representative may be biased and simply deal differently with minorities. Whenever in the pre-employment interviews (or thereafter) minorities are treated unlike other applicants, that is disparate treatment. No systemic discrimination is involved—the action is just illegal.

The manner in which the initial contact is handled may make for a disparate effect in terms of which applicants will go through the selection process. And this of course influences the validity of the selection procedures as well as the appropriateness of the process itself. For example, if no minority persons apply and the selection process is developed over time to differentiate between successful and unsuccessful white or male applicants, the process may well be inappropriate for minorities and females. Or if it is designed to differentiate among experienced workers, it may treat young and inexperienced applicants disparately.

11. The Employment Interview Applicant Evaluation

"In this step, the applicant is being measured and judged on various aspects. This phase may include psychological tests, a physical examination, a security check, detailing of experience, or a personal interview. For lower-skilled occupations, the evaluation process generally is relatively standard, the applicant is measured with many tools. At lower skill levels, the employer frequently considers himself to be the buyer of the job seeker, not the seller of the job opening. . . .

"Different treatment in this step can occur in three ways: (1) providing instructions that are inadequate for some persons; (2) providing tasks or examinations that differ depending on the examiner, the size of the workload, etc.; (3) providing different physical conditions for some applicants than others (for example, having some applicants display their talents on a poorer machine than other applicants).

"After the measuring has been done, each of the interviewers relays his interpreted measurements to some decision-maker who compares the measurements against the criteria established, evaluates the labor market, determines when the organization needs the employees and makes a decision on employment. The decision will include whether to hire at this time and if so, under what conditions. If the decision is not to hire at this time, the applicant may be rejected or, alternatively, he may be placed in a 'hold' pool with other applicants for possible employment at some later point in time...."

Comment: The major expression of bias that can occur here is the use of different criteria for different groups of applicants. More of a given attribute may be required for racial or religious minorities or for women, to cite one example. A more subtle form of discrimination is to defer filling the position if an "undesirable" applicant is not screened out by the established criteria and to go on searching for a "more fully qualified" applicant. This can be a realistic and nondiscriminatory act, or it can be a discriminatory one, depending on the labor market and the degree of performance to be expected from a "better" applicant.

12. The Making of an Employment Offer

If the evaluation is favorable, the applicant is hired. The process is completed.

Forms of systemic discrimination similar to those discussed in the above illustrations for the recruiting or hiring process may be present in the other parts of the personnel process, such as training, evaluation, and promotion. The self-audit described in Part II is meant to identify these.

REMEDIAL ACTIVITIES

A properly conducted audit, complete with a summary report prepared for the use of top management, provides employers with

- an assessment of the precise degree of under- or overutilization of minorities and women in *all* components or groups, departments, functions or occupational categories, and levels of the organization;
- a listing of the personnel system's procedures and criteria that have a disparate effect;
- an evaluation as to whether, and to what extent, the protected classes can be said to suffer the present effects of past discrimination;
- a measure of any sex/wage disparities by job categories (for example, a preliminary inference of possible violations of the Equal Pay Act of 1963);
- at least a preliminary identification of areas of "poor management" that could perhaps be viewed as discrimination.

With such data, top management has an answer to the question whether the corporation is discriminating. In addition the audit provides management with a very useful planning instrument. It generally opens the way to reevaluation of personnel procedures so as to bring to an end the disparate effect of existing procedures. It also leads to the development of a new Affirmative Action Plan or revision and amplification of the existing one. The quantitative part of the audit becomes, in essence, the utilization analysis required as one of the component parts of all affirmative action plans. Furthermore, the quantitative analysis (or utilization analysis) is the basis for formulating the goals and timetables component of an Affirmative Action Plan.*

The launching of remedial programs is the next step. Effective programs are responsive to clearly established needs of existing situations; they generally involve basic personnel or management practices that affect the organization as a whole. Programs geared exclusively to minorities and women are rarely effective and indeed are themselves rarely free of disparate effect. Here the justification for the programs must be that they focus on equal employment opportunities for *all* employees.

In this section the results of audits conducted thus far are reviewed to serve as a basis for the audit in your organization. Also discussed is the issue of "making the worker whole" and the cost of not doing so. Criteria of effective remedial programs are presented as part of a discussion of the failure of past affirmative action programs. Two central points emerge. First, remedial programs need to be tailor made; second, a precise identification of the cause of disparate effect is all that is needed to develop the remedial activity.

TYPICAL FINDINGS OF SELF-AUDITS

The following pattern seems to be characteristic of company self-audits.

1. The employment penetration of minorities as a group is significant in most large corporate establishments. Few firms are very far from matching overall proportional participation of minorities in their work force with the minority proportional participation in the civilian work force of the local employment area. Similarly, except in situations where most employees are blue collar workers, women as a group are employed in significant numbers. Thus the output of an audit seldom leads to the requirement for across-the-board hiring of minorities or women.

2. Analyses of written personnel policy statements and personnel manuals rarely indicate that the policies can in themselves be viewed as leading to disparate effects. Audits generally uncover situations of systemic discrimination which, in the view of corporate management, can just as well be perceived as poor personnel practice. This experience with audits reconfirms the wisdom of personnel experts who have always argued that systemic discrimination is inherently the by-product of "slippage" in management. What managers can do in such a case is insist that departures from written directives involving minorities and women be spelled out and justified in writing.

3. Of the various minorities, the number of blacks is generally closer to proportionality than that of other minorities; the number of Spanish-surnamed Americans (population parity only) or other minorities does not seem to fall into any pattern. Interviews with employers suggest that there is little understanding of the legal requirement of proportionality in the employment of each minority class, not just minorities as a group.

---

*See *Legal Aid Society of Alameda County vs. Brennan* for a comprehensive discussion on the required component parts of an Affirmative Action Plan.

4. Minority employment penetration in most companies is a relatively new phenomenon, and promotion procedures and criteria rely heavily on longevity in employment. Minorities are generally underrepresented in the higher grades or steps of most lines of progression, as well as in the higher occupational categories.

Audits almost always reveal underrepresentation of minorities in most job classifications other than those at points of hire. Women generally are even more underrepresented in job categories other than clerical. Such situations may lead to findings of a broad pattern of discrimination.

Interviews have indicated that, in the main, employer representatives understand equal employment opportunities to mean equality in hiring practices alone. This is clearly not so. The pervasiveness of discrimination in promotions is attested to also by the EEOC's own statistics (see Box 5), and the courts have repeatedly established that parity between total internal work force participation and labor area participation, and aggressive minority recruitment and hiring do *not* protect the employer from findings of discrimination in placement or promotion.

Remedial activities are typically structural. Most often, three things are required: (a) redefinition of lines of progression, which may involve the renegotiation of collective bargaining agreements; (b) the consolidation of senority rosters; (c) the establishment of promotion criteria that are truly job-related.

In situations in which the audit established that minorities or women have been disparately affected by existing procedures, remedial activities may involve identifying minority group members and women who are immediately promotable; offering jobs at higher grades or steps to such individuals as soon

---

5

Of the most recent employer suits brought by EEOC, 120 involved more than one issue:

Hiring practices	63%
Promotion practices	57%
Job classification	49%
Placement practices	46%
Recruitment practices	30%
Pre-hire or promotion criteria	27%

as a vacancy develops; providing fair trial periods to the occupants of the newly filled jobs; "red circling" wage rates to any newly promoted individuals whose earnings in the previous jobs were higher than those in the new jobs.

To remedy the situation when there is a clear presumption of discriminatory promotion criteria may require that the employer make whole those individuals who have been adversely affected by such practices. Fast-track internship or management training programs for minorities and women are effective remedies when the jobs to which these employees are to be promoted require special skills or a particular body of knowledge.

5. The audit often reveals very uneven distribution of minorities across operating departments or functional divisions besides differences of utilization by grade and occupational classification. Not uncommonly, departments with a high proportion of minorities have been "inferior" departments with fewer promotion possibilities, more onerous work, lower status, and a lower average departmental wage. Such situations develop either because of different hiring criteria or because the higher turnover of such departments has made it possible to hire more members of minorities; in certain instances such concentration of minorities is the unexpected by-product of specific affirmative action or hardcore placement programs.

Whatever the origin of different departmental utilization patterns they provide the EEOC with prima facie justification for issuing a charge of broad pattern of discrimination by members of the department as an affected class. The EEOC's record in bringing such cases to the courts has been a successful one; the courts have usually accepted the notion that minority workers and women who have been placed in such departments are to be made whole for wages lost and have ordered employers to pay back wages and legal fees. (See Box 6.)

Interviews with employers have indicated that the issue of departmental overutilization is particularly vexing and misunderstood. Employers complain that they are in trouble both when they hire minorities and when they do not. Part of the problem is that the *placement* of workers is perceived as the *business's business*—as indeed it is if there is reason for it. On the other hand, audits have repeatedly revealed that the concentration of minorities in inferior departments is unjustified because it is neither a job-related requirement nor a business need.

Some employers argue that this concentration of women and minorities results from the expressed desire of applicants for positions in such departments. Experience has shown that such expressions of preference are unwittingly triggered when interviewers tell applicants where minorities and women are currently employed or when they give incomplete descriptions of available jobs. Both situations have been held to be evidence of systemic discrimination.

Remedial activities for cases of departmental imbalances are (a) reevaluating and changing departmental placement criteria; (b) training interviewers in the proper manner of eliciting applicant placement preference; and (c) initiating departmental transfers as described in the situation involving disparate

6

Until the 1972 Amendments, how far back in time back pay might extend was determined on a case by case basis. In *Schaeffer* v. *San Diego Yellow Cabs, Inc.,* for example, the Ninth Circuit Court ordered the defendant to pay attorneys' fees and back pay from the time he became aware of both a trial court's and an EEOC finding of reasonable cause which rendered the "sex-oriented" state labor legislation invalid and unenforceable. Had there been no reliance on the existence of such state legislation, the award would undoubtedly have reached quite further back. Good faith reliance by an employer, for example, on state legislation limiting the hours of employment for female employees was held to be an affirmative defense to a Title VII action.

As it was, the court in *Schaeffer* rejected the defendant's contention that back pay should not be ordered for the time the district court's ruling was on appeal.

The 1972 Amendments did narrow the scope of the back pay remedy by limiting it to two years prior to the filing of a charge of discrimination with the EEOC. While there had previously been no such specific limitation, it in fact will not change the type of awards courts had been ordering, particularly considering that back pay awards will include the time during which the charge is being processed through the Commission.

While Section 706(g) was intended to provide relief for charging parties, section 706(k) allows court discretion to award reasonable attorneys' fees to prevailing parties, plaintiff or defendant, as part of the costs. Given the condition of most charging parties, however, and Congressional priority given to charging parties' vindicating their statutory rights, awards of attorneys' fees to prevailing defendants are not the general rule. . . .

From EEOC's *Annual Report for 1972*

promotions. As indicated in point 4, the remedy here may have to include the payment of back wages. Such payments are rarely welcome news to management. But it is better for management to rectify a personnel malpractice than to have such action forced upon it by the courts. What is more, the EEOC theory of relief interprets remedies to be required only when they do not involve an excessive burden.

In addition to these typical findings, a well-implemented audit usually uncovers a set of conditions representing unobserved and unjustified departures from stated personnel policy.

In a great many cases, particularly among white collar employees, audits have brought to light instances of individuals paid wages not within the stated pay range for their grade or job classification, individuals with inappropriate job titles, lack of comparability between assessments of promotability and patterns of promotion, and so on. Such situations are properly and simply described as poor personnel practice. When minorities and women are involved, they can be perceived by investigators and by the courts as discriminatory.

Whether they will in fact be deemed acts of discrimination is in the ultimate analysis a matter of precedent and court interpretation. What is clear is that not acting on such findings, or not acting vigorously enough on the ground that it is only poor personnel practice, is itself bad management. If nothing else, it heightens the probability that disgruntled employees will bring individual charges of discrimination against the company.

JUSTIFIABLE STATISTICAL DISPARITIES AND OTHER ISSUES

The congressional history of Title VII clearly indicates that discrimination can never be proved by statistics. Furthermore the courts, in all decisions following *Griggs* v. *Duke Power,* have made clear that employers are never required to hire or promote the unqualified or the less qualified. Thus disparate effect creates the presumption but not the proof of systemic discrimination.

Business Necessity

So far in the EEOC's experience, most defenses based on statutory exemptions in behalf of business necessity have been found inappropriate, particularly when the discrimination affects minorities and women. More often than not, genuinely presented defenses are in reality deeply held social prejudices that are not supported by scientific data or empirical tests. In the cases following *Griggs* v. *Duke Power,* the courts have spoken clearly on the impact of business necessity, and since that decision in 1971 the courts have made a very narrow construction of the Bona Fide Occupational Qualification (BFOQ) exemption.

Thus many widely held beliefs as to proper jobs for women—such as line managers usually offer as excuses when an audit reveals a case of disparate effect—are invalid because they reflect social prejudice, not job-relatedness. A number of contentions about the employment of women commonly presented by line management are cited in Box 7. Each of these, as the EEOC reported in 1972, was separately found invalid.

7

Some line management assertions about the employment of women that do not make for a BFOQ exemption:

It is not good management to have girls supervising girls.

The (male) job of outside salesman is too dangerous and unpleasant for females.

Women have poorer attendance records than men.

We would need to construct separate facilities.

The presence of females would create a morale problem.

Our jobs require too much heavy lifting.

Customers would not accept advice from female sales persons.

Availability

Insufficient minority representation in an employer's applicant flow and in the higher occupational classifications is often justified with assertions that qualified candidates are not available. The quantitative differences in the employment of minorities and women may be the result of differences in the availability of qualified candidates, but this rarely happens, and such situations are acceptable only when they can be justified by statutory exemptions.

Almost every personnel man contacted in the survey referred to earlier has, at one point or another, said that if competent minority workers were available, the company would utilize them in proper fashion. Such claims generally do not hold water. Where such situations exist, management should keep in mind:

— the "chilling effect" of past discrimination (examined in detail in Box 8);
— that titles such as manager reflect *internally* defined characteristics; unlike many technical and professional occupations that have externally established and generally accepted skill and knowledge requirements (accountant, radiologist, electrical engineer), the criteria for managerial titles are always open to challenge as to job-relatedness;
— that the situation can be remedied by instituting fast-track promotions and management training programs for currently employed women and minority group members who have demonstrated a potential for growth.

Chilling effect and affirmative action

The EEOC is especially concerned with the chilling effect which past discrimination by employers and unions has had upon the present willingness of qualified minority group members and women to apply for jobs from which they have traditionally been excluded. The extent to which Title VII requires affirmative action to eliminate this effect of past discrimination is still an unsettled question. But it is noteworthy that where an employer or union has a particularly poor hiring record and therefore a particularly bad reputation within minority group communities, Title VII may require the imposition of recruitment goals in order to "break the chain of discrimination."

MAKING THE WORKER WHOLE

Where the courts have found discrimination of the kinds that the audits help reveal, they have ruled that remedies must open the doors to equal employment for all and in addition *must* "make whole" or make restitution to all those who are affected by past discrimination. In practice, this has resulted in very expensive back pay assessments and legal costs.*

What kind of remedial affirmative action the courts have ordered has varied in nature and scope, depending on the kind of discrimination found. They have required fundamental changes in all aspects of employment systems and have specified numbers or percentages of minorities and women to be hired, trained, or promoted in specific job categories, in line with specific goals. They usually require an employer to undertake action quickly, with follow-up monitoring by the court.

Following are five examples of practices ruled discriminatory by the courts, the costs to the employers, and the remedial affirmative actions ordered.

1. In 1971, Anaconda Aluminum Company was ordered to pay $190,000 in back wages and court costs to 276 women who had been maintained in sex-segregated job classifications. While jobs formerly classified "female" and "male" had been reclassified "light" and "heavy," women still were prevented from transferring to heavy jobs. The court ordered the employer to offer the better-paying heavy jobs to women who could qualify.

*For greater detail on court-ordered remedies, see *Equal Employment Opportunity and Affirmative Action, A Guidebook for Employers on Voluntary Action to Comply with the Law,* EEOC, November 9, 1972.

2. Virginia Electric Power Company was ordered to pay $250,000 to compensate black workers for wages they would have earned if they had not been kept from promotion by a discriminatory system. Having found a high school diploma (or equivalent) and aptitude tests not job-related, the court ordered them eliminated as hiring or promotion criteria for blue collar jobs. It also ordered the elimination of existing transfer and promotion systems based on job and departmental seniority (which perpetuated effects of past discrimination). Further, the court ordered the introduction of upward mobility based on total employment seniority. Affirmative hiring was also ordered; at least 25 percent of new union hires were to be nonwhites, until their level of employment in union jobs reached 21.5 percent. Goals were also set for clerical jobs.

3. Black employees of the Lorillard Corporation were awarded $500,000 in back pay when the court found that departmental seniority and limited transfer rights restricted access of blacks to most jobs. Employees who had suffered loss of promotional and pay-raise opportunity were compensated according to what they would have received, based on company seniority, had the discriminatory practices not existed. The company was ordered to establish plantwide seniority and to assure that no employee transferring to a department from which he had been excluded would receive a wage cut. Company and union were ordered to change seniority and assignment systems to assure that blacks had equal opportunity for assignment and promotion to all jobs.

4. The Household Finance Corporation paid $125,000 to 175 white collar female employees who charged they were denied promotions because of sex. Under terms of a consent decree, the company also agreed to hire women for 20 percent of branch representative openings (subject to their availability) until such representatives were 20 percent female and to hire 20 percent from specified minority groups for clerical, credit, and branch representative jobs until total employees reach 65 percent of their population in the labor area. A training program to prepare female and minority employees for better jobs was also ordered.

5. Libbey Owens Ford Company agreed, under a consent decree, to open bidding for all jobs to women, including those previously barred because of state laws requiring overtime pay and weightlifting restrictions. The company and its union agreed to start a training program to aid women employees in transferring to better jobs, to undertake specific recruitment and advertising to attract women applicants, and—depending upon availability— to select women for two out of the next four foremen's jobs in certain departments.

The criteria that the courts developed for compensating workers for past discrimination provide the employer that has carried out the self-audit with a preliminary assessment of corporate liability if its practices are challenged successfully by the EEOC. These criteria are also the bench marks of the costs of making the workers whole through a voluntary compliance agreement.

If a company moves on its own to "restore the rightful economic status" of those affected by internal procedures that are found to have disparate effects (and does so quickly), it can obviously save the large costs of litigation, as a minimum. It should be noted that Title VII (as amended) contemplates back pay to a maximum of two years prior to the time when discrimination is identified. In the foregoing examples, the cited amounts were high because of lengthy investigation, attempted conciliation, and litigation.

THE CHARACTERISTICS OF REMEDIAL ACTIVITIES

Once the audit has established the crucial shortcomings of the personnel system, the task facing the personnel administrator is to identify and recommend ways by which minorities and women can more equitably participate in the work force. Doing so appears difficult. Government assistance has so far been largely confined to the preparation of administrative guidelines and directives. Experience in the area is limited, and checking with another company often proves fruitless.

Yet the fact is that remedial activities are not hard to develop; knowing the right question means knowing the right answer. Indeed, if it is established, for example, that few minority employees are promoted because the "pool" from which promotions are drawn has few minority members, the remedy is to enlarge that pool. If, conversely, the pool contains many minority employees but the promotional criteria create a disparate effect, then the criteria must be reevaluated and modified as appropriate.

The initiating of remedial activities is rarely limited by technical boundaries. It involves primarily the proper application of well-known personnel policies and practices. What appears most useful is to put together the elements of a remedial program in direct response to what the self-audit uncovers. Developing a remedial program is a painstaking process because it must be responsive to specific conditions. There are no model off-the-shelf remedial programs; each must be tailor-made. All that can be done is to list the program ingredients that seem to have the greatest likelihood of success.

Affirmative Action Programs

As defined in Revised Order No. 4, an affirmative action program is a written description of a "set of specific and results-oriented procedures to which a contractor commits himself to apply every good-faith effort. . . . An acceptable affirmative action program must include an analysis of areas within which the contractor is deficient in the utilization of minority groups and women, and further, goals and timetables to which the contractor's good-faith efforts must be directed to correct the deficiencies and thus to increase materially the utilization of minorities and women at all levels and in all segments of his work force where deficiencies exist."

An affirmative action program, to meet the OFCC guidelines of Revised Order No. 4 (and Revised Order No. 14, which is directed to the affirmative action plan review staff of compliance agencies), must be based on and accompanied by a Utilization Analysis as defined in these orders. (See p. 73 for the pertinent section in Revised Order No. 4.) The OFCC-required Utilization Analysis is essentially the same as the audit described in Part II of this book, except that this audit goes further in examining *why* certain disparate effects occur than the Revised Orders require.

Once the areas of over-/underutilization have been identified by the analysis, the setting of goals and timetables, as called for by the Revised Orders, is a comparatively simple matter (if the expected future vacancy rates are taken into consideration). The goals are the achievements of parity in each unit of the organization in each job classification. The timetable establishes the rates at which the goals can realistically be achieved, bearing in mind availability, education and training facilities in the community and the firm, and expected vacancies in each unit and at each level.

Box 9 contains statements from Revised Order No. 4 relating to the nature of goals and timetables and supporting data.

9

Goals should be significant, measurable and attainable....

Goals should be specific for planned results, with timetables for completion....

Goals, timetables, and affirmative action commitments must be designed to correct any identifiable deficiencies....

Goals may not be rigid and inflexible quotas ... but must be targets reasonably attainable....

Support data for the required analysis and program ... will include, but not be limited to, progression line charts, seniority rosters, applicant flow data, and applicant rejection ratios indicating minority and sex status.

Revised Order No. 4 also states than an Affirmative Action Plan, to be acceptable, must establish responsibilities for implementation of the program and must contain descriptions of how the organization plans to develop and execute action-oriented programs to eliminate problems and to reach its goals and objectives. A further major requirement is that an internal audit and reporting system must be implemented to measure the effectiveness of the total program as described in the Affirmative Action Plan.

In summary, an Affirmative Action Plan must contain, on an organizational-unit and job-class basis,

— an analysis of work force utilization in comparison with the external labor area;
— identification of problem areas;
— a statement on goals and timetables for rectifying deficiencies in protected-class utilization and for overcoming such problems;
— stated procedures and programs whereby the goals and timetables and solutions can be achieved.

Voluntary Compliance Agreements

The Equal Employment Opportunity Commission encourages employers to enter into Voluntary Compliance Agreements (VCA). A VCA is first and foremost a voluntarily made contractual commitment to take certain specific steps to do away with aspects of systemic discrimination uncovered by the employer through an audit procedure.

From the Commission's point of view, entering into a VCA is a way of fulfilling its statutory mission. From the employer's point of view, entering into such an agreement is useful because the costs of litigation and penalties are reduced or avoided, the employer avoids any admission of guilt, and the employer who complies with the agreement is protected in carrying out the activities agreed upon in the goals and timetables statement.

Furthermore, if the employer negotiates the VCA under the guise of conciliation, the data presented as part of the conciliation process cannot be used by the Commission if later, or upon lack of agreement, it chooses to level charges of discrimination.

The quid pro quo for the employer commitment is the Commission's contractual obligation not to levy charges of systemic discrimination against the employer. The duration of the agreement is spelled out in the negotiations that precede it and usually spans the period covered by the goals and timetables agreed upon for remedial activities.

Employers should clearly understand that the Voluntary Compliance Agreement deals primarily with systemic discrimination/class action cases. The agreement does not protect the employer from charges of discrimination which are the result of a specific act directed at a specific person and are based upon race, color, religion, sex, or national origin.

There is no major difference between an Affirmative Action Plan and a VCA. The VCA filed with the EEOC may contain the Affirmative Action Plan required by the compliance agency. Both call for:

1. Identification and description of systems and/or subsystems and features of such subsystems found to be discriminatory (narrative statement of issues).
2. Statement of conclusions based upon analysis of the extent to which the features of the employment system have been found to have a disparate effect upon minorities (narrative statement and statistical tables).

3. Specific methods and procedures to be introduced to eliminate systemic discrimination.
4. Projected performance over time, including overall goals and increments of performance to be achieved in significant periods during implementation of the agreement (narrative statement and statistical tables).
5. Reporting/monitoring systems and procedures, including schedules: how data are to be reported and/or monitored; ongoing visits by EEOC or compliance agency personnel; and, if appropriate, statements of exceptions and/or clauses applicable to the specific agreement.

CRITERIA FOR EVALUATING THE EFFECTIVENESS OF REMEDIAL PROGRAMS

Affirmative Action Plans have had a history of achieving less than was expected. They have tended not to conform to the Revised Orders guidelines of "specific and results-oriented procedures" but, rather, to be "soft" even though no doubt well intentioned. Studies by Humanic Designs staff* have suggested the following characteristics of programs with high-yield actions.

1. *They have a visible quantifiable effect.* The programs are directly aimed at producing a specific number of job placements. An in-house training program to prepare top-rated minority craftsmen for vacant or soon-to-be-vacant supervisory positions possesses this characteristic. An after-hours general education program to expand the academic achievement of minority employees does not.

2. *They are informed by an identified company inadequacy rather than an assumed job-applicant or employee deficiency.* The affirmative action is generated by the identification of a company policy or practice which inhibits the hiring or promotion of minorities and women. Given the clear absence of women in a specific department, a company would have two options. The first is to examine and modify the appropriate job classification as well as placement and bidding procedures which could be operating to prevent women employees from gaining the work experience required to perform in that department. The second is to assume that women are neither able nor inclined to undertake a lengthy program of orientation and training aimed at preparing them for that type of work. The first course of action possesses the relevant characteristic; the second does not.

3. *They require observable changes in fundamental policy or practice.* The affirmative action modifies company policies which control the rules governing employment. A job classification seniority system, delineated in a collective bargaining agreement, may effectively prohibit minorities from transferring to lines of progression consisting of higher-wage, higher-skill jobs. A hard affirmative action would be the introduction of plantwide senority as the controlling factor in transfer and promotion.

*For an expanded presentation, see O. A. Ornati and A. Pisano, "Affirmative Action: Why Isn't It Working?" in *The Personnel Administrator*, September/October 1972, pp. 50–52.

4. *They are recurring rather than incidental.* The newly instituted practice or activity is to become a standard operating procedure in the company personnel function rather than an isolated effort. A repeated and established practice of recruiting for entry-level, technical job classifications at predominantly minority trade or vocational schools has this characteristic, as does the planned, ongoing utilization of minority executive placement professionals. A speech on equal employment opportunity by a woman executive to the graduating class of a business school does not.

5. *They are related to precise, numerical goals established in consonance with business needs and objectives.* The affirmative action's anticipated output, a number of minority or female placements, is an integral part of the total manpower forecast. The program goal, probably for a particular occupational category (exempt, or level I management, or whatever) is established in consideration of production requirements and projected vacancy rates and is therefore integrated with company manpower forecasting procedures. More often than not the opposite is true; the goal setting is influenced by the company's traditional inability to employ minorities or women in certain classifications, and it is carried out through informal negotiations between company EEO specialists and line managers after the total manpower needs have already been determined.

6. *They are related to job placement criteria.* The substance of the affirmative action concerns job placement requirements such as education, skill training certifications, and testing. Eliminating from the requirements for a machine operator a grade 12 mathematics level as demonstrated on a standard achievement test illustrates this characteristic. In contrast are procedures typically called minority skill inventory systems. Rather than modifying or eliminating questionable requirements, these identify which minorities possess which particular traits and may very well screen out minority candidates more efficiently than was done in the past. It may be that the real need is to examine the relevance of the criteria instead of going far afield to find women or minority group members who meet the criteria.

PART II

PART II

THE SELF-AUDIT

The methodology in this section was developed on the basis of four major inputs: (1) the experience of carrying out investigations in industrial environments; (2) the translation into operative directives of criteria embodied in Commission documents such as *The Theory of Relief* and *Proving Discrimination*; (3) the translation into operative directives of criteria embodied in court decisions and in related court-ordered remedies; (4) discussions with the Technical Assistance Division Staff of the EEOC Office of Voluntary Programs. The self-audit establishes a procedure for uncovering systemic discrimination as it is defined by Commission policy and as it would have to be organized for legal review. The procedure is thus precise, and each step in it is important.

As described earlier, the materials are organized into seven units which build successively one upon another. The first two units, or sections, provide guidance in the collection of the data. These sections involve no analysis; they are the building blocks of later work. The third unit deals with measurements of parity. It provides the user with the first and most general element of statistical evidence in identifying the presence of discrimination. Nothing in this unit helps "prove" discrimination. On the other hand, it may provide the user with a way of deciding whether the investigation should be continued. Indeed, should the indices of population parity and occupational parity derived from carrying out the described activity stand at or near 100, one may argue that systemic discrimination is not significant.

The fourth section guides the user into later activities by identifying specific employment practices; the section also permits the establishment of priorities for later work and helps in preliminary identification of possible major compliance issues.

The fifth and sixth sections establish the steps necessary for the identification of discrimination in recruitment, hiring, promotion, transfer, and termination. Here the work prepared for in the first three sections is put to use in documenting discovery of systemic discrimination. Section 7 applies the principles of the "theory of relief" and directives of Revised Order No. 4 in developing specific remedies and in setting goals and timetables.

The internal organization of the sections is uniform. Each has three main parts: (1) a general statement; (2) the statement of an objective that describes the expected outcome of the activity; and (3) a detailed statement of procedures to be followed.

The pages that follow provide step-by-step guidance in the necessarily complex process of carrying out a self-audit. It is suggested that this guide be given a first reading from beginning to end. Each section should then be worked out in detail, with the described activities carried out in sequence. It is recognized that a complete audit will take a considerable amount of work and will be time-consuming, but with use and familiarity, several things will become clear: (1) Many activities can be carried out simultaneously. (2) There are time lags in the availability of data, and these periods can be used for other activities. (3) Much of the work of data collection, particularly in unit 1, can be done by computer if one is available.

The utilization of the work force is to be assessed by determining the number and proportion of employees who are members of each sex and sex-within-race, as well as (1) the percentage *participation* of each class in the relevant organizational units and job titles or job groups,* in the EEO-1 categories,[†] and in pay grades within units; (2) the percentage *distribution* of each class over units, job titles/groups, and so on.

These pages present a manager's view of the steps in a compliance audit. It will be appreciated that many points of detailed procedure are omitted because they would only obscure the outline. In any case, these detailed procedures are contingent upon such varying factors as the organizational structure and the data storage and retrieval mechanisms in use. Organization-specific methods should therefore be designed within the parameters set out here.

One final word of caution is in order. The law respecting equal employment opportunity is continually being refined; it behooves every manager to keep up to date on the legal requirements described in Part I and to reflect these requirements in his organization's audit methods.

---

*Job groups are combinations of job titles which represent work of a closely similar nature and which are in the same pay grade. Such job titles are merged when the number of incumbents in a title is too small or when the number of titles is too large for separate analyses. In either case, it is permissible to merge titles only if they are truly similar in content and pay level.

[†]The nine EEO-1 categories are: officer/manager, professional, technician, sales worker, office/clerical, craftsman, operative (skilled and semiskilled workers), laborer, service worker.

1. CLASSIFYING THE WORK FORCE

1.1 General All organizations consist of functional and administrative units through which they operate. The designations given to such units, and their nature and characteristics, will depend on several factors, among which are size and type of product or service. Most often, designations are made in terms of functions or activities, such as product development, marketing, manufacturing, sales, financial control, and personnel; administrative or managerial descriptions, such as division, department, and line of progression; facilities, such as plant or office.

The audit has to be conducted for each separate facility; for each organizational entity that has responsibility for hiring, placing, promoting, transferring, or terminating; and for each line of progression. The term "unit" refers throughout to all such facilities, responsibility centers, and lines of progression.

1.2 Objective Identify all functional and administrative units of the organization and all job titles, including a wage designation for each job title.

Identify the number (as of the most recent available date) of each of the following in each unit and in each job title: total; total male; total female; Caucasian, male and female; Negro, male and female; Oriental, male and female; Spanish-surnamed American, male and female; American Indian, male and female.

1.3 Procedure Most organizations maintain charts and lists which identify the organizational units. These and other documents also name job titles, usually coded with an identification number for payroll and other personnel data maintenance purposes. Collective bargaining agreements are a source of job titles, especially those classified as nonexempt. Assemble this information and review it to become familiar with the specific terminology and descriptions the organization employs to identify units and job titles.

The utilization (that is, the participation and distribution) of the protected classes in the organization's work force must be shown in a series of tables known as Work Force Classification Tables. These tables must be prepared so as to display the number of employees, in total and in each of the 12 sex and sex-within-race groupings, within each organizational unit being studied (which will include the total organization, individual establishments and other responsibility centers, down to departments within establishments if they have personnel process responsibilities). These numbers are distributed in various ways:

1. over job title, or group of titles where homogeneity of pay and content justifies such grouping. Such titles/groups are ranked in ascending or descending order of pay grade and mean/median wage/salary within grade.
2. (a) pay grades, or, if pay grades are wide,
   (b) narrower pay ranges, chosen to avoid the loss of information that could obfuscate disparate wages/salaries for members of the protected classes when wide pay grades are used.
3. EEO-1 categories and pay grades.

The numbers of employees so distributed can be represented by percentages in two ways:

(a) By expressing the numbers of employees who are of a given sex or a given sex and race, and who also belong to a given job title/group (or pay grade/range or EEO–1 category), as a percentage of the total in that same job title/group (or pay grade/range or EEO–1 category). This gives the percentage *participation* of the given protected class in the given classifications. Participation percentages are computed for each sex and sex-within-race group for the same major classifications. Figure 1(a) shows the percentages of the total in both pay grade and job title, and Figure 1(b) shows the percentages of the total in EEO–1 categories and pay grades.

(b) By expressing the number of employees who are of a given sex or a given sex and race, and who also belong to a given job title/group (or pay grade/range or EEO–1 category), as a percentage of the total employees in the same sex or sex-and-race class. This gives the percentage *distribution* of the protected class with respect to the job title/group (and so on). Distribution percentages are computed for each sex and sex-within-race group and for all job titles/groups, pay grades/ranges, and EEO–1 categories. In other words, in a rectangular matrix, displaying the incidence of members of sex and sex/race classes with respect to jobs, pay grades, and so on, with columns displaying the classes and rows displaying the jobs, pay grades, or other such status categories, horizontal percentaging (on row totals) gives percentage *participation* and vertical percentaging (on column totals) gives percentage *distribution*. Figure 2 shows the percentages of the members of a given protected class in a given pay grade and job title.

Figures 1 and 2 illustrate how an employer might go about setting up the forms for displaying the data for his organization, using, of course, actual, appropriate titles, pay ranges, and so on. These participation and distribution tables, which are generated for the entire organization and its separate units, constitute the data base for identifying underutilization and overutilization of the protected classes. The participation data are used, in particular, for comparison with the corresponding data on the external labor market. EEO–1 category data (and to some extent major job title/group data) can be compared by means of parity indices described in section 3.

Whenever the corresponding external labor area data cannot be identified, the detailed distribution and participation data by job title, job group, and pay grade are interpreted through direct comparison of the utilization of one class with another within the organizational unit itself. Distribution tables show the type and level of work performed by each class and hence whether there is an undue concentration of women or minorities in particular job titles, organizational units, or pay grades. Participation tables show the relative penetration of the classes into the various types and levels of jobs and hence whether the representation of a particular class or classes is, for example, unduly high in the less-skilled, less-well-paying jobs and unduly low in the more-skilled, better paid jobs.

Another analysis that is helpful in assessing the utilization of the protected classes is the mean or median wage or salary paid per year to members of each class, qualified by length of service. (See Figure 3.) In other words,

Figure 1(a).   Sex and race participation rates by pay grade and job title/group.

Pay Grade	Job Title/ Group	Total Employees	Total M	Total F	Caucasian M	Caucasian F	Negro M	Negro F	SSA M	SSA F	Oriental M	Oriental F	Am. Ind. M	Am. Ind. F
	FOREMAN III													
	Number	2	2	–	2	–	–	–	–	–	–	–	–	–
	Participation %	100.0	100.0		100.0									
15	FOREMAN II													
	Number	4	4	–	4	–	–	–	–	–	–	–	–	–
	Participation %	100.0	100.0		100.0									
	FOREMAN I													
	Number	4	4	–	4	–	–	–	–	–	–	–	–	–
	Participation %	100.0	100.0		100.0									
All grade 15														
	Number	10	10	–	10	–	–	–	–	–	–	–	–	–
	Participation %	100.0	100.0		100.0									
14														

Pay Grade	Job Title/ Group	Total Employees	Total M	Total F	Caucasian M	Caucasian F	Negro M	Negro F	SSA M	SSA F	Oriental M	Oriental F	Am. Ind. M	Am. Ind. F
	LOADER													
	Number	50	45	5	20	2	10	2	15	1	–	–	–	–
	Participation %	100.0	90.0	10.0	40.0	4.0	20.0	4.0	30.0	2.0				
1	JANITOR													
	Number	5	3	2	1	1	–	–	2	1	–	–	–	–
	Participation %	100.0	60.0	40.0	20.0	20.0			40.0	20.0				
All grade 1														
	Number	55	48	7	21	3	10	2	17	2	–	–	–	–
	Participation %	100.0	87.3	12.7	38.2	5.5	18.2	3.6	30.9	3.6				
All grades/jobs														
	Number	127	100	27	68	10	12	10	20	7	–	–	–	–
	Participation %	100.0	78.7	21.3	53.5	7.9	9.5	7.9	15.7	5.5				

Figure 1(b). Sex and race participation rates by EEO-1 categories and pay grades.

EEO-1 Category	Pay Grade		Total Employees	Total		Caucasian		Negro		SSA		Oriental		Am. Ind.	
				M	F	M	F	M	F	M	F	M	F	M	F
Officials/ Managers	21	#	5	5	–	5	–	–	–	–	–	–	–	–	–
		%	100.0	100.0		100.0									
	20	#	8	6	2	6	2	–	–	–	–	–	–	–	–
		%	100.0	75.0	25.0	75.0	25.0								
	19	#	12	12	–	11	–	–	–	–	–	1	–	–	–
		%	100.0	100.0		91.1						8.9			
	18	#	40	38	2	36	1	2	1	–	–	–	–	–	–
		%	100.0	95.0	5.0	90.0	2.5	5.0	2.5						
All Officials/Managers		#	65	61	4	58	3	2	1	–	–	1	–	–	–
		%	100.0	93.8	6.2	89.2	4.7	3.1	1.5			1.5			
Service	1	#	17	12	5	9	4	1	–	2	1	–	–	–	–
		%	100.0	70.6	29.4	52.9	23.5	5.9		11.8	5.9				
All Service		#	17	12	5	9	4	1	–	2	1	–	–	–	–
		%	100.0	70.6	29.4	52.9	23.5	5.9		11.8	5.9				
All EEO-1 Categories		#	460	171	289	143	222	12	37	11	21	5	9	–	–
		%	100.0	37.2	62.8	31.1	48.3	2.6	8.0	2.4	4.6	1.1	1.9		

44

Figure 2. Sex and race distribution rates by pay grade and job title/group.

UNIT: *Production and Maintenance*

Pay Grade	Job Title/ Group	Total Employees	Total M	Total F	Caucasian M	Caucasian F	Negro M	Negro F	SSA M	SSA F	Oriental M	Oriental F	Am. Ind. M	Am. Ind. F
15	**FOREMAN III**													
	Number	2	2		2	–	–	–	–	–	–	–	–	–
	Distribution %	1.6	2.0		2.9									
	FOREMAN II													
	Number	4	4	–	4	–	–	–	–	–	–	–	–	–
	Distribution %	3.2	4.0		5.9									
	FOREMAN I													
	Number	4	4	–	4	–	–	–	–	–	–	–	–	–
	Distribution %	3.2	4.0		5.9									
All grade 15														
	Number	10	10		10	–	–	–	–	–	–	–	–	–
	Distribution %	7.9	10.0		14.7									
14														
1	**LOADER**													
	Number	50	45	5	20	2	10	2	15	1	–	–	–	–
	Distribution %	39.5	45.0	18.5	29.4	20.0	83.3	20.0	75.0	14.3				
	JANITOR													
	Number	5	3	2	1	1	–	–	2	1	–	–	–	–
	Distribution %	4.0	3.0	7.0	1.5	10.0	–	–	10.0	14.3				
All grade 1														
	Number	55	48	7	21	3	10	2	17	2	–	–	–	–
	Distribution %	44.5	48.0	28.5	30.9	30.0	83.3	20.0	85.0	28.6				
All grades/jobs														
	Number	127	100	27	68	10	12	10	20	7	–	–	–	–
	Distribution %	100.0	100.0	100.0	100.0	100.0	100.0	100.0	100.0	100.0				

UNIT: *Production and Maintenance*

EEO-1 Category	Seniority	Total Employees	Total		Caucasian		Negro		SSA		Oriental		Am. Ind.	
			M	F	M	F	M	F	M	F	M	F	M	F
Officials/ Managers	1 year	$15.0	$15.0	–	$15.0	–	–	–	–	–	–	–	–	–
	2 years	15.5	15.5	–	15.5	–	–	–	–	–	–	–	–	–
	3 years	16.0	16.0	–	16.0	–	–	–	–	–	–	–	–	–
	• • •													
	10 years	20.0	20.0	–	20.0	–	–	–	–	–	–	–	–	–
Service	1 year	6.5	7.25	6.0	7.5	7.0	–	–	6.0	–	–	–	–	–
	2 years	6.0	–	6.0	–	–	–	–	–	6.0	–	–	–	–
	3 years	–	–	–	–	–	–	–	–	–	–	–	–	–
	• • •													
	10 years	8.0	8.0	–	8.5	–	–	–	7.5	–	–	–	–	–

the mean wage or salary of individuals within a class is calculated separately for groups of comparable seniority. These statistics are computed separately for facilities and for job categories within facilities.* As in the case of the detailed distribution and participation data, interpretation here is by comparison of the mean/median wage or salary of one class (of comparable seniority) with that of the other classes (EEO-1 categories and/or job titles or groups).

*A more sophisticated approach is to use the statistical technique of multiple regression analysis, in which the independent variable would be mean wage/salary and the dependent variables would include membership of a protected class and seniority. Thus the effect of class membership upon wage/salary can be determined, all other things being equal.

2. CLASSIFYING THE POPULATION OF THE EXTERNAL LABOR AREA

2.1 General Revised Order No. 4 defines the labor area as the "area surrounding the facility" or the "area in which the (organization) can reasonably recruit." The Department of Labor's Manpower Administration defines it as a "central city or cities and surrounding territory within commuting distance . . . an economically integrated geographical unit within which workers may readily change jobs without changing their place of residence . . . (an area to coincide with those boundaries)." This can be translated into the Standard Metropolitan Statistical Areas (SMSAs) used by the Bureau of the Census.

It should be noted that the June 1974 decision in the *Legal Aid Society of Alameda County v. Brennan* case (Judge J. D. Zirpoli, U.S. District Court, Northern District of California) has more narrowly defined the parameters to be used by an employer in determining the external labor area. It was ruled in this case that an Affirmative Action Program must adopt as its labor area the SMSA, county, or city (of the SMSA) which has the highest (proportional) minority population unless there is an appropriate justification for another selection.

For the present analysis, two sets of data are required (for use in section 3, Measuring Parity). One set of data is to show the representation of the protected classes in the civilian work force of the labor area in which the organization is located; the other is to show the representation of the protected classes in occupational categories, as listed in the Employer Information Report (EEO-1) (and in job categories where such data are available) within the same labor area.

2.2 Objective Identify and collect external labor area data.

2.3 Procedure Two major sources may be consulted, the EEOC and the Bureau of the Census. The EEOC publication is *Job Patterns for Minorities and Women in Private Industry.*

The 1970 census figures on employment are presented in a series entitled *General Social and Economic Characteristics PC (1)-C.* It is made up of 53 reports, one for the United States and one for each state, the District of Columbia, and Puerto Rico. The census questions divide race into several groups: Caucasian; Negro; American Indian; and Japanese, Chinese, Filipino, Hawaiian, and Korean, which the EEO-1 Report groups as Oriental. Further questions on mother-tongue also produced statistics for Spanish-speaking persons.

Tables compiled from the data collected in the 1970 census include statistics on employment by race and sex as well as by place of employment and method of transportation to work. (These statistics are useful in determining the area from which an employer can draw his work force.) Statistics on educational attainment and vocational training are also organized by race and sex, and these can provide a reasonable assessment of the number of minority group members and women who might qualify for certain jobs that have specific educational requirements. Statistics are also presented for unemployed persons, giving the reason for leaving and the occupational category of the last job by race and sex.

The volumes for the individual states (for example, *General Social and Economic Characteristics Series PC (1)–C6, California*) list all the information cited earlier by race and sex for the SMSAs, central cities, counties, and rural areas of the state. Employment status and type of occupation are presented separately for each minority group by SMSA and central city, by county, by towns and places, and by parishes in which at least 400 of the minority group resided at the time of the census.

The Bureau of the Census also publishes other series which might be useful sources of statistics on minorities for a specific area. One of them, called *Employment Profiles of Selected Low-Income Areas PHC (3) Series*, is made up of 76 reports covering 51 cities and 7 sets of rural counties. This series is especially important to an employer in a poverty area. It presents such data as employment statistics, educational attainment, vocational training, job history, and, specifically for the unemployed, data about the desire for work, educational attainment, last job category, and reason for leaving.

Series PC (SI) consists of two final reports based on the 1970 Census of Population which contain data about Negro population: *Report 1–Distribution of the Negro Population by County* and *Report 2–Negro Population in Selected Places and Selected Counties.* Similar reports are available for the Spanish population, for the Japanese, Chinese, and Filipino populations, and for the American Indian population.

Where possible, the census data should be updated. The department for the Continuing Population Survey provides broad trend data for the larger areas; along with this, state and city Departments of Labor sometimes conduct specific studies which can be helpful in bringing some 1970 census data up to date.

3. MEASURING PARITY

3.1 General Interest in parity stems from the use of the concept by the courts. In dealing with matters of discrimination, particularly when resolving questions of fact, the courts have always looked at the general pattern of employer conduct. As part of the pattern, they have looked at the composition of the employer's work force. In addition, the courts have found it appropriate to consider statistics about the labor force participation of minorities and women in a geographic area to infer the existence of a pattern or practice of discrimination. Marked disparities have been viewed, not as proof of discrimination, but as prima facie evidence of discrimination.

Revised Orders No. 4 and No. 14 also make clear that Affirmative Action Plans, to be acceptable to federal agencies, must be based on utilization analyses which compare the internal participation of minorities and women with their availability in the external labor area.

Purpose. Parity measures identify statistical disparities in the representation of the protected classes in job titles/categories, EEO–1 categories, and other selected units (department, line of progression, plant, and so on) when compared with labor area data.

To some extent, statistical disparities represent the cumulative effect of an organization's personnel practices. They therefore provide some focus for the analyst, because they spotlight areas in which the personnel practices may be discriminatory. For example, a statistical disparity in the representation of a protected class in the occupational category "technician" would indicate that specific personnel practices used to fill job titles in that category, whether in recruitment and hiring or promotion and transfer, may be discriminatory and need to be analyzed in detail.

Types. Two types of parity are to be measured. The first is population parity, in which the participation of the protected classes in the various major organizational units* and in total are compared with their participation in the civilian work force of the external labor area. The comparison is expressed as an index: a numerical value showing the ratio of internal participation to external participation of a protected class. Thus the measure of population parity is called the "index of population parity."

The second type to be measured is occupational parity. For this measure, the participation of the protected classes in the organization and all relevant units of the organization, in occupational categories (as named in the Employer Information Report EEO-1), and in job categories for which corresponding external labor market data can be obtained is compared with their participation in the same categories in the external labor market. Again, the comparison is expressed as an index, and this measurement is called the "index of occupational parity."

3.2 Objective Compute indices of population and occupational parity for the protected classes.

3.3 Procedure Identify the various units and EEO-1 occupational categories and job categories for which an index is to be computed. Compute population indices for the total organization and for each unit previously identified as a responsibility center. Compute occupational indices for each EEO-1 category (and for each job category where this is possible) for each unit.

NOTE: As the 1970 census data become increasingly out of date, the comparatively detailed occupational breakdowns available from the census series are less and less acceptable. The EEO-1 categories are probably somewhat less sensitive to change, but with the passage of time the EEOC reports, even though they are based on incomplete data, will probably provide a better picture of reality for SMSAs. (Finer breakdowns are not available from EEOC.) At the date of publication of this book (1975), it is doubtful whether categories finer than EEO-1 categories are appropriate for internal/external participation comparisons, except where a job group is so critical in assessing an organization's performance that even data of dubious validity is better than none. A case in point would be accountants for companies whose business is accounting.

---

*A major organizational unit is one that is (1) responsible for employment, promotion, and transfer, and is (2) large enough to be expected to reflect the population of the labor area.

For the remainder of this text, the term *occupational category* will be used to denote both EEO–1 categories and job categories, whichever is appropriate.

The remainder of section 3.3 gives procedural details for computing the indices, with examples based on data for Negro males found in Figure 1(b). The first step necessarily is to compute the participation rates. It is understood that these calculations must be made for all 12 classes in all organizational units in all job categories.

For each organizational unit, compute an internal participation rate for all employees. This is accomplished by dividing the number of employees in the unit into the number of such employees who are members of each sex and sex/race class, then multiplying by 100 to convert to percentages. In computational form:

$$\text{Internal (unit) participation rate } (P_{IU}) = \frac{\text{No. of class in unit}}{\text{Total no. in unit}} \times 100$$

Example. In Figure 1(b) it will be seen that out of 460 employees in the unit (in that case, an entire establishment) 12 were Negro males. The participation rate is therefore:

$$P_{IU} = \frac{12}{460} \times 100 = 2.6\%$$

This is separately computed for each of the 12 classes.

A similar procedure has to be followed for each occupational category within each organizational unit. The formula is:

$$\text{Internal (occupational) participation rate } (P_{IO}) = \frac{\text{No. of class in occupational category}}{\text{Total no. in occupational category}} \times 100$$

Example. In Figure 1(b), out of 65 officials/managers, 2 are Negro males.

$$P_{IO} = \frac{2}{65} \times 100 = 3.1\%$$

This, too, is separately computed for each sex and sex/race group.

Participation rates computed in this fashion are the percentage entries in tabular displays such as Figure 1 and Figure 2, and the raw numbers used to compute them are the number entries in these displays. In fact, in preparing the Work Force Classification tables, much of the work in computing parity indices has already been accomplished.

In order to compute parity indices, it is next necessary to calculate in similar manner participation rates for the external civilian labor force of the labor area. Using the data as described above in sections 2 and 3.3, proceed as follows: Divide the total number into the number in each class and multiply by 100 to give percentages. The formula is:

External ("population") participation rate (P_{EP}) = $\dfrac{\text{No. of class in area work force}}{\text{Total no. in area work force}}$ × 100

Example. If the number of Negro males in the external labor area is 25,000 and the total civilian labor force in the area is 100,000, then:

$$P_{EP} = \frac{25{,}000}{100{,}000} \times 100 = 25\%$$

This computation is carried out for each class. It will be seen to correspond to that for the internal (unit) participation rate.

Corresponding to the internal (occupational) participation rate is a labor area (occupational) participation rate to be computed in a parallel manner.

External (occupational) participation rate (P_{EO}) = $\dfrac{\text{No. of class in area work force in category}}{\text{Total no. in area work force in category}}$ × 100

Example. If the number of Negro males who are officials/managers in the labor area is 200 and the total number of officials/managers is 10,000, then:

$$P_{EO} = \frac{200}{10{,}000} \times 100 = 2.0\%$$

The computation of the four types of participation rates shown above are preliminary to computing the parity indices.

Index of population parity (IPP). This index permits comparison of the participation of the protected classes per se in the total organization and in the various units of that organization with their participation in the relevant external labor area. It is computed by dividing P_{IU} (computed for the organization/unit) by P_{EP} (computed for the external work force) and multiplying by 100.

Example. If the participation of Negro males in the unit is 2.6 percent and in the civilian labor force of the external labor area is 25 percent, then:

$$IPP = \frac{P_{IU}}{P_{EP}} \times 100$$

$$= \frac{2.6}{25.0} \times 100$$

$$= 10.4$$

Index of occupational parity (IOP). This index compares participation in the organization of the protected classes in a given occupational category with their participation in the same occupational categories of all employers in all industries in the labor area.

To compute the index of occupational parity (IOP), divide P_{IO} by P_{EO} and multiply by 100.

Example. Where the participation of Negro males in an organization's officials/managers category is 3.1 percent (P_{IO}) and in the external labor area it is 2 percent (P_{EO}), the index is computed as:

$$IOP = \frac{P_{IO}}{P_{EO}} \times 100$$

$$= \frac{3.1}{2.0} \times 100$$

$$= 155$$

Organize all the indices in one table. (See Figure 4.)

Figure 4. **Measures of parity table.**

	IPP	IOP
Negro males in the XYZ facility, to Negro males in the population of the external labor area (SMSA)	10.4	
Negro males in the occupational category officials/managers to Negro males in the occupational category officials/managers in the labor area		155
Spanish-surnamed American males in the production department, to Spanish-surnamed Americans in the population of the external labor area (SMSA)	10	

As stated earlier, the measurement of parity, expressed as an index, reflects to some degree the cumulative effects of personnel practices. It is the first and most general element of statistical evidence in identifying the presences of discrimination.

Perfect parity is expressed as an index of 100. Any index lower than 100 shows a statistical disparity. Obviously, the greater the difference, the greater the disparity. Any index higher than 100 also shows a statistical disparity. In this case, the interpretation of the disparity depends not only on the size of the difference, but also on the nature of the comparison. For example, an index of 155 for Negroes in the officials/managers category would not usually be regarded as prima facie evidence of discrimination, while an index of 150 for females in the clerical category would be so regarded. This is because of the well-established tendency of employers to overutilize minorities and women in lower-level jobs and to underutilize them in higher-level jobs and the underlying premise of equal employment opportunity legislation, that minorities and women are the classes who need protection under law.

4. PREANALYSIS: CLASSIFYING PERSONNEL PRACTICES AND COMPLIANCE PROBLEMS

4.1 General Personnel practices are all policies, procedures, and so on that affect job placement (recruitment, hiring, promotion, transfer, and termination), that affect wages and salaries, and that affect all other terms, conditions, and privileges of employment.

Personnel practices are usually developed and maintained by an organization in relation to some level, status, or other category of employment. Most organizations classify their personnel practices in terms of exempt or nonexempt. Exempt is a status covering job titles excluded from the wage and hour provisions of the Fair Labor Standards Act (FLSA). These are usually executive, administrative, and professional positions. Nonexempt job titles are covered by the provisions of the Act.

Thus in a typical situation there will be two recruitment/hiring practices and two promotion/transfer practices, exempt and nonexempt. One can also expect to find different wage and salary structures for each of the categories. It should be noted, however, that there may be other categories of employment for which separate personnel practices are maintained. Examples of such categories and divisions are professional and nonprofessional; managerial and nonmanagerial; monthly salaried and hourly.

In this section each personnel practice that applies to a specific employment level, status, or other category is to be identified. Also to be identified in this section are the personnel practices governing the terms, conditions, and privileges of employment (grievance procedures, facilities, maternity benefits, and so on) as distinguished from those governing job placement (recruitment, hiring, promotion, transfer, and termination).

Compliance problems may be any past or present issues, action, and the like that suggest possible violations of Title VII. Therefore, the identification and classification of major problems in the section provide some direction and priority for the analyses of later sections.

4.2 Objective Identify each discrete personnel practice that applies to a specific level, status, or other category of employment. Identify personnel practices governing the terms, conditions, and privileges of employment. Identify major compliance problems.

4.3 Procedure *Classifying personnel practices.* Documents to be collected and examined include, but are not limited to, personnel policies and procedures manual and all other written statements of personnel policy and procedure; Affirmative Action Plan, as required by Revised Order No. 4; collective bargaining agreements; employment application forms; employment manuals used by personnel specialists and interviewers; employee performance evaluation forms. Such documents will be useful resources in classifying discrete personnel practices. Interviews with personnel representatives are another source of information. The purpose of an interview should be clearly stated: to identify or name the discrete practices, rather than to conduct detailed analysis of the specific activities within the practice.

Identifying employment practices governing the terms, conditions, and privileges of employment. Examine written statements, such as the personnel policies and procedures manual and the collective bargaining agreement. Interview personnel representatives, who in this case will probably be employee benefits and wage-and-salary specialists. Abstract pertinent rules and procedures in each of the following areas:

Absenteeism	Holidays, vacations, leaves of absence
Appearance and dress	Hours of work, shift differentials,
Rest periods	overtime
Discipline	Insurance, welfare plans
Facilities	Retirement
Grievances	Marital status, maternity benefits

For some of the items, quantitative data would be useful. For example, in the case of discipline one could identify and compare the incidence of disciplinary actions for selected classes.

Review all EEOC and OFCC guidelines which are related to these personnel practices in order to determine whether the policies and rules governing the practices are in consonance with such guidelines.

Classifying compliance problems. In order to make an initial classification of compliance problems, pertinent records and reports of compliance activity should be reviewed. Analyze this information (for example, types of charges) to determine the employment areas in which issues have arisen, such as recruitment, hiring, or promotion. If the organization has an Affirmative Action Plan available it may describe problems, at least from the organization's perspective.

A visual inspection in the form of a tour of selected facilities will provide a broad assessment as to where certain classes of employees appear to be concentrated or absent.

Interviews with representatives of agencies that deal with employment referral and the like, and are located in the area surrounding an employing facility of the organization, may bring to light special issues concerning protected class referrals.

Interviews with selected employees, including union representatives, may also be a source for problem identification. The number of employees interviewed should be small (no more than five); the employees should be selected from different levels (supervisory, managerial, and so on); and the questions should be open-ended.

Interviews with operating or line managers (heads of production departments, for example, as distinguished from staff employees such as personnel representatives) are an additional source of information to be considered.

Summarize all the preceding information in a chart and list. (See Figure 5.)

Figure 5. Classification of personnel practices.

Personnel Practice	Employment Category
1. Recruitment and hiring	Clerical, technician, and all other nonexempt jobs.
2. Recruitment and hiring	All exempt jobs.
3. Promotion/transfer	All jobs covered by the collective bargaining agreement.
4. Promotion/transfer	All jobs outside collective bargaining agreement provisions except for promotions into supervisory or managerial positions.
5. Promotion/transfer	All managerial and supervisory positions.

Classification of Compliance Problems

Preanalysis shows evidence of the following compliance problems:

1. Identifying sources of protected class applicants in the external labor area, for professional job titles.
2. Identifying positions into which female employees may be promoted from clerical job titles.
3. Procedures through which supervisors assess the promotion potential of employees.
4. Questions delineated on the application form which do not appear to serve a business need.

5. ANALYZING PERSONNEL PRACTICES AND IDENTIFYING DISCRIMINATION: RECRUITMENT AND HIRING

5.1 General *Definition.* Recruitment and hiring are the two elements of the procedure through which individuals are identified as applicants for, and are placed into, entry-point jobs. Such jobs are predominantly filled from outside the organization—in other words, from the external labor market. Like all personnel practices governing job placement, each recruitment and hiring practice consists of a series of specific steps or activities through which individuals move.

Basic questions. The basic question in *recruiting* is whether the applicant flow generated by the recruiting process has a sex and race composition matching that of the appropriate external labor area(s). This is therefore another parity issue. (Note that there may be more than one, since if there are "ports of entry" for professional and managerial jobs—that is, if there are distinct entry-level jobs for these types of employees—the labor area appropriate to such employees is likely to be regional and sometimes national.)

The availability of jobs may be limited by restrictions maintained by the organization, or it may be limited by the inadequacy of the means of recruiting. An example of organizational restriction is the exclusive use of referral sources which do not include qualified protected class members. An example of inadequate means is word-of-mouth recruiting, whereby the employed work force is made aware of job openings and generates the applicant flow. Should the work contain few protected class members, the net effect of such an activity would be to restrict the class of persons to whom the jobs are made available.

The basic question in *hiring* is to ascertain whether the selection criteria applied in any activity of the practice (application processing, interviewing, testing) produce a statistical disparity between the applicant race and sex composition and the race and sex composition of the newly hired employees.

5.2 Objective Analyze each recruitment and hiring practice which has been identified. Identify factors which contribute to a statistical disparity and do not serve a legitimate business need.

5.3 Procedure *Identification of entry-point job titles.* Review the classification of personnel practices prepared in section 4 and note the employment category to which the recruitment and hiring practice applies. For this employment category, identify the entry-point job titles. One of several ways of doing this is to identify the prior status of each incumbent in every job within the category and determine which jobs have incumbents who were hired from the external labor area. Another means of identifying entry-level jobs is to interview a personnel representative, review each job title within the employment category, and have this individual identify each job title which is predominantly filled from the external labor area. If this method is followed, it would be appropriate to randomly sample the incumbents' personnel records for the job titles so identified and ascertain whether these employees were in fact hired from the external labor force. Also, documents such as the collective bargaining agreement may identify entry-point job titles. Whatever the precise means, identify the job titles for most of the entry-point placements, which are governed by the recruitment and hiring practice under consideration.

Materials documentation. All forms and written statements of personnel policy and procedure that are related to and descriptive of the recruitment and hiring practice should be included as part of this analysis.

Description of the practice. Prepare a description of the recruitment and hiring practice, listing each activity within the practice—for example, issue application forms to walk-in applicants; collect and review applications; distribute applications among interviewers; interview applicants; review file of job requisitions; test applicants; make offer of employment. The description should also identify the purpose or anticipated outcome of each activity—for example, interview applicants in order to elicit interest and determine relevance of education, training, and work experience. Interviews with personnel representatives and observation of employment office procedures will provide the required information.

Measuring the quantitative performance of the practice. Quantitative performance consists of the numbers of each employee class who are affected by each activity of the practice. It is in this performance that a statistical disparity for the protected classes is to be determined. Request (1) applicant data for the entry-point job titles under consideration for at least the past 12 months, organized by class; (2) hire data for the applicants, organized by class and by job title assignment. Where a test has been identified to be a selection mechanism, data on the number tested and the test results are to be collected and organized by class.

Measuring applicant rates. Using the aforementioned applicant data, compute a participation percentage (P_A) for each class:

$$P_A = \frac{\text{No. of class applicants}}{\text{Total no. of applicants}} \times 100$$

Measuring hire rates. Using the aforementioned hire data, compute a distribution percentage (D_H) for each class:

$$D_H = \frac{\text{No. of class hired}}{\text{No. of class applicants}} \times 100$$

Measuring placement rates by job title/job group assignment. Again using the hire data, compute a distribution percentage (D_P) for each class and for each job title/job group:

$$D_P = \frac{\text{No. of class hired into job title}}{\text{No. of class hired}} \times 100$$

Where possible, data showing the quantitative performance of each activity should be collected. The extent to which such data are available depends upon the organization's personnel records maintenance. The special usefulness of these data is that they show the specific activities that produce the disparity.

Organize the data of this section in a table such as Figure 6.

Identification of selection criteria. Selection criteria consist of any and all characteristics, traits, or conditions used by the organization in deciding who is to be hired or promoted. They may fall within a range characterized by a formal test at one end and a general assessment of maturity at the other end. Although there will be a discrete recruitment and hiring practice for a specific employment category, selection criteria vary according to the entry-point job titles. For example, a recruitment and hiring practice for the non-exempt category will almost certainly show different selection criteria for entry-point draftsmen and electrical maintenance men. Written statements of personnel policy and procedure and interviews with personnel representatives, especially employment interviewers (and department heads or managers who have been identified as making final selection decisions), will serve to delineate selection criteria. These sources of information are to be supplemented by the following procedure.

(a) Review the information concerning selection criteria that has been obtained by examining written statements of personnel policy and procedure and by interviewing personnel representatives. Define the general categories

Figure 6. Analysis of recruitment and hiring practices.

From _____ 19 ___ to _____ 19 ___

	Total	Total		Caucasian		Negro		SSA		Oriental		Am. Ind.	
		M	F	M	F	M	F	M	F	M	F	M	F
I *Applicants*													
Number	1000	1000	–	900	–	50	–	50	–	–	–	–	–
Participation %	100%	100%		90%		5%		5%					
II *Hires*													
Number	600	600	–	580	–	10	–	10	–	–	–	–	–
Distribution %	60%	60%		64%		20%		20%					
III *Job Titles*													
(Number and distribution %)													
Job Title A	200	200	–	193	–	–	–	–	–	–	–	–	–
	33%	33%		33%									
Job Title B	200	200	–	193	–	–	–	–	–	–	–	–	–
	33%	33%		33%									
Job Title C	200	200	–	194	–	10	–	10	–	–	–	–	–
	33%	33%		33%		100%		100%					
IV *Quantitative Performance of Activities*													
(Number and distribution %)													
Receive applicants	1000	1000	–	900	–	50	–	50	–	–	–	–	–
Preliminary interview	1000	1000	–	900	–	50	–	50	–	–	–	–	–
	100%	100%		100%		100%		100%					
Complete application	1000	1000	–	900	–	50	–	50	–	–	–	–	–
	100%	100%		100%		100%		100%					
Employment test	1000	1000	–	900	–	50	–	50	–	–	–	–	–
	100%	100%		100%	–	100%		100%					
Employment interview	640	640	–	600	–	20	–	20	–	–	–	–	–
	64%	64%		67%		40%		40%					
Investigation of personal history	610	610	–	580	–	15	–	15	–	–	–	–	–
	61%	61%		64%		30%		30%					
Referral to department	600	600	–	580	–	10	–	10	–	–	–	–	–
	60%	60%		64%		20%		20%					
Department interview	600	600	–	580	–	10	–	10	–	–	–	–	–
	60%	60%		64%		20%		20%					
Offer of employment	600	600	–	580	–	10	–	10		–	–		
	60%	60%		64%		20%		20%					
Hire	600	600	–	580	–	10	–	10		–	–		
	60%	60%		64%		20%		20%					

in which the selection criteria could be classified. Consider four categories: education, job-related training, job-related experience, and applicant job preference.

(b) Obtain and examine the personnel records of the incumbent employees in the entry-point job titles under consideration. In each of the four categories, identify the condition, trait, or characteristic shown or possessed by each incumbent. Consider a random sample where the number of incumbents is so large that an examination of all personnel records is impractical.

(c) Summarize the selection criteria. An example of a useful summary format is as follows:

76% of the incumbents have completed eight or more years of school.

57% of the incumbents have had job-related training.

41% of the incumbents have had job-related experience.

83% of the incumbents stated a preference for a type of work related to the entry-point job.

After this analysis of a recruitment and hiring practice has been completed, the analysis is to be examined for discrimination. Primarily, this will involve comparing the data which have been organized, and making assessments about the causes of identified disparities between the classes.

Statistical disparity in the participation of the protected classes in the entry-point job titles to which the recruitment and hiring practice applies. Earlier in this section the entry-point job titles were identified. For the sum of these job titles, compute a participation percentage (Y_1) for each protected class, where P_1 represents the number of the protected class in the job titles and P_2 represents the total number of employees in the job title.

$$Y_1 = \frac{P_1}{P_2} \times 100$$

A participation percentage for each protected class in the external labor area was computed in section 3. Compare the two percentages. Any difference showing a larger participation for the protected class in the external labor area than in the job titles represents a statistical disparity. This is a first element of evidence that the recruitment and hiring practice is discriminatory. The entry-point job titles being considered are part of a larger unit or occupational category for which an index of parity was prepared in section 3. If the index is below 100 for minorities or women, the statistical disparity in entry-point participation may represent part of the total divergence from parity.

Statistical disparity in the quantitative performance of the recruitment and hiring practice for the protected classes. Examine the recruitment and hiring data in Figure 6.

(a) The participation percentage of the protected class applicants should be compared to the participation percentage of the protected class in the external labor area (computed in section 3). Any data which show a larger participation for the protected class in the external labor area than among applicants represent a statistical disparity. This is a second element of evidence that the recruitment activities are discriminatory.

(b) The distribution percentage of the minority and female class hires should be compared to the distribution percentage of the appropriate comparison class (usually Caucasian males). Any data which show a smaller distribution percent for the protected class represent a statistical disparity. This is a third element of evidence that hiring activities are discriminatory. If data showing the quantitative performance of each activity within the practice are available, compare distribution percentages to identify the specific activities that produce statistical disparities.

(c) The distribution percentage of a protected class, for the individual job titles into which hires were placed, should now be compared to the distribution percentage of the appropriate comparison class. Any data which show that fewer of the protected class hires are placed into certain jobs represent a statistical disparity. This is a fourth element of evidence. This particular disparity, especially when it occurs in relation to entry-point job titles which require similar qualifications, suggests that although protected class members are hired, they may be assigned to less desirable positions. Therefore, when this kind of disparity is noted, steps should be taken to assess the comparative desirability of the job titles under consideration. These steps include visiting the work site to observe working conditions; examining wage and salary schedules; examining the specific promotions and transfers during the past year from these job titles, in order to assess the nature of promotional opportunity. In this case, these are basic questions: Do protected class members perform dirtier or more strenuous work? Do they earn less? Are there fewer promotions, or are the promotions made to different jobs which are also less desirable? Is there a narrower range of jobs into which they can be promoted? Data which show whether the protected classes have fewer or less desirable promotion opportunities are collected and analyzed in section 6.

Activities and selection criteria contributing toward the statistical disparities. Review the activities and selection criteria which have been described for this recruitment and hiring practice. Delineate the factors contributing to the disparities. Such factors represent the causes of discrimination, or the precise means through which discrimination operates, as distinguished from their statistical effects (disparities). They comprise a fifth element of evidence and are the specific elements of systemic discrimination to which remedies or corrective actions need to be addressed. Their delineation may require the identification and analysis of additional data. For example, if word-of-mouth recruiting has been assessed as one factor contributing to a disparity, select at random a number of applications for the job titles under consideration, and determine how many show an employee as the referral source. Another example is a situation in which a specific selection criterion has been identified, such as the completion of a technical course at a vocational school. Here three sets of data would be relevant. One is the personnel records of incumbent employees, to find out whether they have had such training; another is external labor market data, to estimate the degree to which members of the protected class have had such training; the third is interviews with rejected applicants or current employees, to determine whether protected class members have had the training yet have been denied employment.

Absence of evidence that a legitimate business need is served by the factors identified as contributing to a disparity. It is up to the organization to demonstrate the business need of factors which contribute to statistical disparities in the quantitative performance of a personnel practice for the protected classes. The question is: Are such factors related to job performance or essential to the conduct of the business? Consider the following analysis.

(a) Identify the major activities of the job title for which there are disparities. As sources of information, use position descriptions, collective bargaining agreements, observation of job performance, interviews with supervisors and employees.

(b) Match the criteria and the major job activities. Assess the business need of the criteria. Keep the following in mind: Criteria consisting of demonstrated performance of an activity that is part of the job will probably meet the test of business need; criteria which are believed to predict the ability to perform the activity, such as height and weight requirements, are more suspect.

(c) Consider these additional points. Do all employees in the job title possess the criteria qualifications? If not, the criteria are suspect. Are the criteria applicable to jobs above the level being examined, but not to that job? This is sometimes used as a justification for applying such criteria, the argument being that they are necessary for promotion. This is not an acceptable defense for using excessively stringent criteria.

(d) Where formal testing produces a statistical disparity for a protected class, there are two questions. First, is the test valid—that is, does it measure what it purports to measure? Second, if the test is valid, is the characteristic or ability being measured essential to the conduct of the business? Is the cut-off score that is being used at a realistic level?

The lack of evidence that the factors identified as contributing to a disparity serve a legitimate business need is a sixth element of evidence of discrimination.

Statistical significance. The statistical disparities in the quantitative performance of a personnel practice, for a protected class, may be due to chance and therefore not be of statistical significance. According to EEOC's *Guidelines on Employee Selection Procedures*, statistical significance of a disparity (the difference between a distribution percentage for a protected class and for a comparison class) "ordinarily means that the relationships should be sufficiently high as to have a probability of no more than 1 to 20 to have occurred by chance." Thus the standard is set at the .05 level of significance. A formula for determining the statistical significance of a given disparity can be found in any standard reference on statistical techniques. Consider making this determination in each case where the disparity involves the largest numbers of people.

6. ANALYZING PERSONNEL PRACTICES AND IDENTIFYING DISCRIMINATION: PROMOTION, TRANSFER, AND TERMINATION

6.1 General *Definition.* Promotion, transfer, and termination are the practices through which incumbent employees are placed in other job titles or other units of the organization and through which employees leave the organization by reason of resignation, dismissal, work force reduction, retirement, or death.

61

The jobs governed by promotion and transfer practices are predominantly filled from inside the organization. In section 4 it may have been determined that there is more than one promotion, transfer, and termination practice.

Basic questions. One question in promotion and transfer has to do with the class of persons to whom jobs are made available. Such persons comprise the candidate pool, drawn from the internal labor market. Selection from this pool may involve restrictions of two kinds.

The first kind of restriction is due to the way in which parts, segments, units, or pools (each of them consisting of specific job titles and referred to here as relevant labor pool) of the internal labor market are defined as providing the incumbency, experience, and other characteristics required for promotion or transfer to other specific job titles.

For example, if an organization asserts that a foreman position in a maintenance department is generally filled by promoting from a journeyman classification in that same department, it has defined the relevant labor pool of the internal labor market for the maintenance foreman job title. If the protected classes are not represented in the journeyman classifications of that department, a restriction has been imposed upon the classes to whom the job is made available.

The second kind of restriction is due to the way in which notifications of promotional opportunities are made—in other words, the job posting and bidding procedures.

Another basic question is whether the selection criteria (including seniority) applied in any activity of the practice—test, supervisory interview and evaluation, or whatever—produce a statistical disparity for the protected class candidates in the relevant labor pool.

There are several basic questions relevant to Title VII in terminations. First, do members of protected classes leave the organization (whether voluntarily or involuntarily) at higher rates than the comparison class. Second, where there is a collective bargaining agreement, does the seniority system which regulates layoff produce a statistical disparity for a protected class? Third, in the absence of a seniority system, does the organization utilize other criteria for termination which produce a statistical disparity?

6.2 Objective   Analyze each promotion, transfer, and termination practice which has been identified. Identify factors that contribute to a statistical disparity and do not serve a legitimate business need.

6.3 Procedure   *Identification of job titles filled from the internal labor market.* Review the classification of employment practices prepared in section 4, and note the employment category to which the promotion, transfer, and termination practice applies. For this employment category, identify the job titles which are filled from the internal labor market. As in the case of recruitment and hiring, there are alternative means through which this may be accomplished. Follow the procedure described in section 5.3 for identifying entry-point job titles. However, in promotion, transfer, and termination the personnel records of incumbent employees are examined to determine whether those employees were placed from the internal labor market.

Materials documentation. All forms and written statements of personnel policy and procedure which are related to and descriptive of the recruitment and hiring practice should be included as part of this analysis.

Description of the practice. Prepare a description of the promotion, transfer, and termination practice similar to the one that was prepared for recruitment and hiring (that is, list each activity within the practice and so on).

Identification of relevant labor pools. In some organizations, especially those where labor unions operate and collective bargaining agreements are in effect, the relevant labor pool for a particular job title can be determined by examining the defined and published lines of progression. In other organizations, the relevant labor pools will not be defined and published.

Relevant labor pools can best be determined by identifying the prior job title of each incumbent employee for each job title to which this promotion, transfer, and termination practice applies: (a) Select the job title or job group for which the relevant labor pool is to be defined. For each incumbent employee, identify the prior job title. (b) From the participation rate data such as are shown in Figure 1, identify the number of employees of each sex and sex-within-race for each prior job title and hence, by summation, in the relevant labor pool for the job in question. (See Figure 7.)

Figure 7. Defining relevant labor pools.

	Total	Total		Caucasian		Negro		SSA		Oriental		Am. Ind.	
		M	F	M	F	M	F	M	F	M	F	M	F
Number promoted to maintenance foreman	20	20	–	18	–	1	–	–	–	1	–	–	–
Number in:													
Job Title A	43	43	–	40	–	1	–	2	–	–	–	–	–
Job Title B	61	61	–	50	–	3	–	7	–	1		–	–
Job Title C	120	120	–	100	–	15	–	5	–	–	–	–	–
Total in relevant labor pool	224	224	–	190	–	19	–	14	–	1		–	–

One alternative to describing the relevant labor pool for all job titles to which the promotion, transfer, and termination practice applies is to identify only those specific job titles into which actual promotions were made for the past year.

Measuring the quantitative performance of the practice. As in recruitment and hiring, it is in this performance that a statistical disparity for the protected classes is to be determined. Request the following:

(a) Candidate data for each relevant labor pool under consideration, organized by class. This information is available in the table that was prepared in defining relevant labor pools. Candidates are all persons in the relevant labor pool.

(b) Promotion data, for at least the past twelve months, organized by class and by job title assignment.

(c) Termination data, for at least the past twelve months, organized by class and by job titles.

As in recruitment and hiring, where a test has been identified to be a selection mechanism, data showing the number tested and test results are to be collected and organized by class.

Measuring candidate rates. Using the candidate data, compute a participation percentage (P_C) for each class:

$$P_C = \frac{\text{No. of class candidates}}{\text{Total no. of candidates}} \times 100$$

Measuring promotion rates. Using the promotion data, compute a distribution percentage (D_{PR}) for each class:

$$D_{PR} = \frac{\text{No. of class promoted}}{\text{Total no. of class candidates}} \times 100$$

Measuring placement rates by job title assignment. Again using the promotion data, compute a distribution percentage (D_{PJT}) for each class and for each job title:

$$D_{PJT} = \frac{\text{No. of class promoted into given job title}}{\text{Total no. of class promoted}} \times 100$$

Compute separate distribution percentages for test results. Also, where possible, collect data showing the quantitative performance of each activity within the practice.

Measuring termination rates. Using the termination data, compute a distribution percentage (D_{TR}) for each class terminated in the job title:

$$D_{TR} = \frac{\text{No. of class terminated in given job title}}{\text{Total no. of class in the given job title}} \times 100$$

Organize the data of this section in a table such as Figure 8.

Identification of selection criteria. The identification of selection criteria in promotion, transfer, and termination follows the same procedure as in recruitment and hiring. (See section 5.3.) However, particular attention should be paid to the issue of seniority, which is usually a selection criterion in itself.

Figure 8. Analysis of promotion, transfer, and termination practices.

	Total	Total M	Total F	Caucasian M	Caucasian F	Negro M	Negro F	SSA M	SSA F	Oriental M	Oriental F	Am. Ind. M	Am. Ind. F
I Candidates in Relevant Labor Pool													
Number	1000	1000	–	900	–	50	–	50	–	–	–	–	–
Participation %	100%	100%		90%		5%		5%					
II Promotions													
Number	600	600	–	580	–	10	–	10	–	–	–	–	–
Distribution %	60%	60%		64%		20%		20%					
III Job Titles (Number and distribution %)													
Job Title A	200	200	–	193	–	7	–	–	–	–	–	–	–
	33%	33%		33%		70%							
Job Title B	196	196	–	193	–	3	–	–	–	–	–	–	–
	33%	33%		33%		30%							
IV Quantitative Performance of Activities (Number and distribution %)													
Prepare supervisory assessments	1000	1000	–	900	–	50	–	50	–	–	–	–	–
	100%	100%		100%		100%		100%					
Prepare candidate list	640	640	–	600	–	20	–	20	–	–	–	–	–
	64%	64%		67%		40%		40%					
Refer to department	610	610	–	580	–	15	–	15	–	–	–	–	–
	61%	61%		64%		30%		30%					
Department interview	610	610	–	580	–	15	–	15	–	–	–	–	–
	61%	61%		64%		30%		30%					
Offer of position	600	600	–	580	–	10	–	10	–	–	–	–	–
	60%	60%		64%		20%		20%					
Promote	600	600	–	580	–	10	–	10	–	–	–	–	–
	60%	60%		64%		20%		20%					
V Terminations (Number and distribution %)													
Job Title A incumbents	500	500	–	450	–	50	–	–	–	–	–	–	–
Job Title A terminations	35	35	–	30	–	5	–	–	–	–	–	–	–
	7%	7%		7%		10%							
Voluntary terminations	25	25	–	23	–	2	–	–	–	–	–	–	–
	71%	71%		77%		40%							
Nonvoluntary terminations	10	10	–	7	–	3	–	–	–	–	–	–	–
	29%	29%		23%		60%							

Seniority units are discrete industrial groups that take one of these forms: line-of-progression seniority; departmental seniority; plant seniority; industry seniority (found only in highly organized industries). Determine which is the controlling form of seniority for the job titles under consideration. This can be determined by examining the provisions of the collective bargaining agreement governing promotion and transfer. Note that the form of seniority utilized will also serve to define the relevant labor pools for specific job titles. For example, if departmental seniority is the controlling form, the relevant labor pool is defined as only those job titles within a particular department.

Seniority provisions commonly include a statement that the most senior person must also be "qualified." The criteria determining who is qualified will have been already determined. However, it is appropriate to determine whether seniority, whatever the form, is the controlling factor—in other words, whether it is an applied and operative selection criterion. This can be ascertained in a number of ways. Identify the seniority dates of employees who have been promoted into the job titles under consideration during the past year. Compare these dates with the dates of employees who are in the relevant labor pool and therefore could have been considered. In addition, records of employee grievances sometimes include incidents of bypass, when a promotion was granted to a less senior employee.

Identification of selection criteria for promotion in exempt categories is more difficult. Even when such criteria are formally defined in policy manuals they are expressed in broad language permitting diverse interpretations as to who is and who is not qualified. Here the procedures described in section 5.3 are to be followed, noting that job-related experience as a criterion has to be developed in greater detail. Categories to be considered include experience in preparing reports, dealing with outsiders, and buying supplies. For promotions to positions involving supervision of other employees, consideration should be given to the number of individuals supervised in prior jobs and their overall levels of responsibility. After this analysis of a promotion, transfer, and termination practice has been completed, the analysis is to be examined for identifiable discrimination. Again, this will entail comparing the assembled data and making assessments about the causes of disparities.

Statistical disparity in the participation of the protected classes in the job titles to which the promotion, transfer, and termination practice applies. Earlier in this section, the job titles which are filled from the internal labor market were identified. Locate these job titles, and for the sum of these job titles compute a participation percentage (P_{ILM}):

$$P_{ILM} = \frac{\text{No. of class in job titles}}{\text{No. of employees in job titles}} \times 100$$

A participation percentage for each protected class in the external labor area (P_{EP}) was computed in section 3. Compare P_{ILM} with P_{EP}. A larger participation for a protected class in the external labor area than in the job titles filled from the internal labor market represents a statistical disparity.

Statistical disparity in the quantitative performance of the promotion, transfer, and termination practices for the protected classes. Examine Figure 8, which organizes promotion, transfer, and termination data. Check the following data.

(a) The participation percentage of the protected class candidates in each relevant labor pool should be compared to the participation percentage of the protected class in the external labor area (computed in section 3). Any data showing a larger participation for the protected class in the external labor area represent a statistical disparity.

(b) The distribution percentage of the protected class promotions/transfers and terminations should be compared to the distribution percentage of the appropriate comparison class. Any data showing a smaller distribution percent for the protected class represent a statistical disparity. As in the case of recruitment and hiring, if data showing the quantitative performance of each activity within the practice are available, identify the specific activities within the practice which produce statistical disparities by comparing distribution percentages for each activity.

(c) The distribution percentage of a protected class, for the individual job titles into which those promoted were placed, should now be compared to the distribution percentage of the appropriate comparison class. Any data showing that fewer of the protected class are promoted into certain jobs represent a statistical disparity.

Activities and selection criteria contributing to the statistical disparities. Review the activities and selection criteria for this promotion, transfer, and termination practice. Delineate the factors contributing to the disparities that have been identified.

(a) Where a disparity has been identified, and the participation of the protected class candidates is compared in each relevant labor pool and in the external labor area, there may be two contributing factors: limited hiring of the protected class into the entry-point job titles of the relevant labor pool, and/or the way of defining the relevant labor pool (for example, the exclusion from the pool of clerical job titles, predominantly held by females).

(b) Where a disparity has been identified, in comparing the distribution percentage of promotions/transfers for the protected class and the comparison class, a contributing factor may be the kind of seniority utilized, the comparative length of seniority, or the application of criteria such as supervisory performance evaluation and tests.

(c) Where a disparity has been identified, in comparing the distribution percentage of terminations for the protected class and the comparison class, the contributing factors will often be similar to those for promotions/transfers.

In delineating the factors (especially seniority) which produce statistical disparities in promotion, transfer, and termination, a fundamental issue concerns the effect of a past or present practice of exclusion or discriminatory job placement in hiring, where such effect is maintained by the promotion/transfer practice. The issue is illustrated in the following examples.

First, assume that prior to a certain date, an organization did not employ Negroes. Assume further that the refusal to hire was not founded on the supposition that Negroes as a class were incapable of safely and efficiently performing the work. The past practice of exclusion from the work force means that current Negro employees, regardless of their ability to perform the work, will not be promoted into any job title if a qualified Caucasian who was hired prior to that date is seeking the job and if plant seniority is the operative selection criterion. Thus the promotion/transfer practice produces a statistical disparity indicating a present effect of past discrimination.

Second, the organization considers women solely for clerical employment. Where line-of-progression seniority is the operative selection criterion, women will not hold job titles which constitute the relevant labor pools for promotion/transfer into nonclerical job titles. Again, the promotion/transfer practice produces a disparity resulting from the present effect of past discrimination.

Following is the procedure to identify and analyze such an issue.

First, review the statistical disparities which have been identified for promotion, transfer, and termination practices. Identify each relevant labor pool in which the participation percentages of the protected classes are lower than those in the external labor area; identify job titles in which the promotion distribution percentages are lower for the protected classes than for the comparison class.

Second, review the activities and selection criteria which contribute to these statistical disparities, giving special consideration to the form of seniority and the means of defining the relevant labor pool. These are the elements of the promotion/transfer practice which produce a present effect of past discrimination.

Third, examine the table which was prepared for defining relevant labor pools (Figure 7), the Work Force Classification Table (Figure 1a), and the listing of entry-point job titles prepared in section 5 (Figure 6). Identify the entry-point job titles which have the following characteristics: they are part of any relevant labor pool and their participation percentages for the protected classes are below those in the external labor area.* Examine the table which was prepared for the analysis of recruitment and hiring practices (Figure 6). Identify disparities in the quantitative performance of the recruitment and hiring practice which applies to these entry-point job titles. Review the delineation of factors which contribute to these disparities, as well as the assessment of their business need, prepared in section 5. Where there is no evidence of business need, these factors represent the elements of a past or present practice of exclusion or discrimination in recruitment and hiring.

Absence of evidence that a legitimate business need is served by the factors identified as contributing toward a disparity. The principles and procedures for assessing business need in promotion, transfer, and termination are essentially the same as in recruitment and hiring. However, the use of seniority as a selection criterion in promotion, transfer, and termination requires additional considerations.

---

*External labor area data for job titles/groups may not always be available in up-to-date form, as has been pointed out in earlier sections.

First, one of the underlying assumptions of seniority systems is that incumbency or a period of residency in a specific job title or type of work serves to prepare and thereby qualify an employee for performance in another job title. This is especially true in line-of-progression seniority systems. A line of progression is a series of jobs which are connected in such a way that an employee progresses from one job to the next. There are two basic lines of progression. In one, experience on the lower-rated job is necessary to perform the higher-rated job. (That is, the jobs are related by knowledge or skill needed to perform them.) This is a functionally integrated line. Where such is the case, line-of-progression seniority would meet the business need requirement as an operative selection criterion. However, the question may be raised, especially in terms of remedy, as to how long an individual should spend in one job before being considered qualified for the next. A line of progression may not be functionally integrated; it may merely be a group of jobs belonging to the same industrial function or organizational unit, but not related to each other by similar knowledge or skill. Here, line-of-progression seniority would not meet the business-need requirement.

Second, in making an assessment of the business need of a seniority system, examine the job activities data described in section 5. Also, determine whether all employees have been required to follow the line as defined. For the lines of progression and their component job titles under consideration, identify the incumbent employees who have reached or are near the top of a line of progression. Select at random from among the personnel records of these incumbents, and identify all prior job positions to determine what the sequence of progression has been.

Statistical significance. Procedures for determining the statistical significance of identified disparities are the same for promotion, transfer, and termination data as they are for recruitment and hiring data.

Wage and salary schedules. Most promotions and transfers are accompanied by an increase in wage or salary. For nonexempt job titles, and for job titles covered by a collective bargaining agreement, such increases and their size are usually not matters of management prerogative; that is, all employees are likely to be granted the appropriate increase. However, for the exempt job titles this may not be the case.

The size of a salary increase for an exempt employee is for the most part a management prerogative, based upon an evaluation of employee performance, work history, and education. Here the question is whether the protected classes were granted the same increases over the same periods of time as a comparison class; that is, are any differences in average paid rates due solely to merit factors such as performance and length of service?

(a) Examine the Work Force Classification Table and identify the exempt job titles in which there are protected class incumbents.

(b) Examine the personnel records or current payroll records of those who show the same starting or anniversary date of employment, and compute an average salary. In the same way compute an average salary for the comparison class incumbents who show the same anniversary date, and note any differences. (A format such as Figure 3, listing job titles in place of EEO-1 categories, can be used to display the data.)

(c) Where differences exist, ascertain the criteria for salary increases in promotion and transfer, and assess whether such criteria are related to job performance. The performance ratings of individual employees will indicate what the criteria are and what the performance has been.

7. FORMULATING REMEDIES, GOALS, AND TIMETABLES

7.1 General The analysis and identification of systemic discrimination is to lead to the preparation of an Affirmative Action Plan (necessitated by law for contractors to the federal government) or to a Voluntary Compliance Agreement between the organization and the U.S. Equal Employment Opportunity Commission. Revised Order No. 4 (see p. 73) cites the eight points to be looked for in an Affirmative Action Plan. It will be seen that those relating to the utilization analysis are the same as those described in detail in the preceding pages of this text. Voluntary Compliance Agreements should be based on the same criteria. The following objectives and procedures therefore apply to either situation.

7.2 Objective Formulate a remedy for each employment practice in which, as determined in the analysis, the following conditions are present:

— Statistical disparity in the participation of any protected class in the job titles to which the employment practice applies.
— Statistical disparity in the quantitative performance of the employment practice for any protected class.
— Employment practice activities and selection criteria that contribute to the statistical disparities and do not serve a legitimate business need.

7.3 Procedure Through the procedure described here, remedial actions or provisions are to be formulated. Instructions in delineating specific details are omitted because such details will be organization-specific and will therefore vary.

Recruitment and hiring. Review the analysis of section 5, especially the table that organizes the data (see Figure 6), and identify the following disparities where present:

Participation percentage for entry-point job titles.
Participation percentage for applicants.
Distribution percentage for hires.
Distribution percentage for job titles.
Distribution percentage for specific activities.

Identify the factors that contribute to such disparities and do not serve a legitimate business need. List the recruitment and hiring practices assessed to be discriminatory and the protected classes against which they discriminate. Formulate a remedy which is responsive to the discrimination so identified.

Promotion, transfer, and termination. Review the analysis of section 6, especially the table which organizes the data (see Figure 8), and identify the following disparities where present:

Participation percentage for job titles filled from the internal labor market.

Participation percentage for relevant labor pools.

Distribution percentage for promotions.

Distribution percentage for job titles.

Distribution percentage for specific activities.

Distribution percentage for terminations.

Identify the factors that contribute to such disparities and do not serve a legitimate business need. List the promotion, transfer, and termination practices assessed to be discriminatory and the protected classes against which they discriminate. Formulate a remedy which is responsive to the discrimination so identified.

Goals and timetables. The ultimate or long-range goal of all remedial and corrective actions is to achieve approximately the same representation of minorities and women, in all job classifications, as their overall external labor force participation. Job classifications may consist of the major EEO–1 occupational categories, or they may be specific to a particular organization or industry.

A timetable is required to delineate the period within which long-range goals are to be met. It is influenced by turnover (retirements, resignations, dismissals, promotions, transfers) and by the estimated availability of minorities and women in the labor markets inside and outside the company.

The internal labor market, as a source of minority and female candidates, provides for a more explicit assessment of availability than the external labor market, in that the current work force is of a known quality and quantity.

Assessing availability in the external labor market consists of examining the primary sources of labor market information, which describes the status and various characteristics of employers, workers, and potential members of the work force.

In order to estimate the number of a protected class who are available in the external labor market for specific job titles, consider the following: protected class population in the external labor area; specific manpower reports such as monthly reports on levels of employment and unemployment on a regional basis, annual reports of the College Placement Council, and reports of the Engineering Manpower Commission of the Engineers Joint Council; enrollment in high schools, trade and vocational schools and institutes, and colleges; private and public employment agencies; and training facilities that are maintained by the organization (or that the organization is willing to undertake) or those located in the community.

In order to estimate the number of a protected class who are available in the internal labor market for specific job titles, consider the following: protected class population in the relevant labor pools; directories or inventories of employee skills, education, and interests; and organization training resources.

Section 60-2.11
Revised Order No. 4

Based upon the Government's experience with compliance reviews under the Executive order programs and the contractor reporting system, minority groups are most likely to be underutilized in departments and jobs within departments that fall within the following Employer's Information Report (EEO-1) designations: officials and managers, professionals, technicians, sales workers, office and clerical and craftsmen (skilled). As categorized by the EEO-1 designations, women are likely to be underutilized in departments and jobs within departments as follows: officials and managers, professionals, technicians, sales workers (except over-the-counter sales in certain retail establishments), craftsmen (skilled and semiskilled). Therefore, the contractor shall direct special attention to such jobs in his analysis and goal setting for minorities and women. Affirmative action programs must contain the following information:

(a) An analysis of all major job classifications at the facility, with explanation if minorities or women are currently being underutilized in any one or more job classifications (job "classification" herein meaning one or a group of jobs having similar content, wage rates and opportunities). "Underutilization" is defined as having fewer minorities or women in a particular job classification than would reasonably be expected by their availability. In making the work force analysis, the contractor shall conduct such analysis separately for minorities and women.

1. In determining whether minorities are being underutilized in any job classification the contractor will consider at least all of the following factors:

(i) The minority population of the labor area surrounding the facility;

(ii) The size of the minority unemployment force in the labor area surrounding the facility;

(iii) The percentage of the minority work force as compared with the total work force in the immediate labor area;

(iv) The general availability of minorities having requisite skills in the immediate labor area;

(v) The availability of minorities having requisite skills in an area in which the contractor can reasonably recruit;

(vi) The availability of promotable and transferable minorities within the contractor's organization;

(vii) The existence of training institutions capable of training persons in the requisite skills; and

(viii) The degree of training which the contractor is reasonably able to undertake as a means of making all job classes available to minorities.

2. In determining whether women are being underutilized in any job classification, the contractor will consider at least all of the following factors:

(i) The size of the female unemployment force in the labor area surrounding the facility;

(ii) The percentage of the female work force as compared with the total work force in the immediate labor area;

(iii) The general availability of women having requisite skills in the immediate labor area;

(iv) The availability of women having requisite skills in an area in which the contractor can reasonably recruit;

(v) The availability of women seeking employment in the labor or recruitment area of the contractor;

(vi) The availability of promotable and transferable female employees within the contractor's organization;

(vii) The existence of training institutions capable of training persons in the requisite skills; and

(viii) The degree of training which the contractor is reasonably able to undertake as a means of making all job classes available to women.

Principal Terms in the Vocabulary of EEO Compliance

affected class
> A group of people with a common characteristic (race, sex, religion, national origin) who have been denied equal opportunity in violation of Title VII of the Civil Rights Act of 1964. This denial may occur at any step in the employment process: recruitment, placement, promotion, compensation, shift assignment, or others.

Affirmative Action Plan
> A document required of government contractors, under regulations of the OFCC. The employer is obliged to compare the internal distribution of minorities and females to their incidence in the external labor market and to determine whether or not he is at parity with the external labor market. The Affirmative Action Plan is a statement of goals, timetables, and programs indicating how the employer plans to move from his current status to parity.

Bona Fide Occupational Qualification (BFOQ)
> The Civil Rights Act of 1964, Title VII, provides that it is not an unlawful employment practice for an employer, employment agency, union, or joint labor-management committee to engage in any employment practice, other-

These definitions have been created for the layman and are not to be considered definitive.

wise prohibited by the Act, on the basis of the religion, sex, or national origin of an employee, applicant, or apprentice, where religion, sex, or national origin is a bona fide occupational qualification reasonably necessary to the normal operation of the particular business or enterprise. The burden of proof is on an employer who claims, as a defense to charges of discrimination, the exception for a bona fide occupational qualification.

compliance agencies

Organizations established under the OFCC as internal subunits of major government departments or agencies, including, for example, the Atomic Energy Commission, Department of Health, Education and Welfare, Department of Labor. They are charged with the administration of Executive Order 11246, Revised Orders No. 4 and No. 14, and with the collection and analysis of EEO-1 Reports and Affirmative Action Plans. Their powers of enforcement include the ability to deny government business to contractors found in violation.

disparate effect

The result of treatment that is quantitatively different for a protected class or classes than for other employees in an organization or in its subunits, within job titles, pay grades, or other aspects of employment. Disparate effect is generally a result of the application of criteria or standards of acceptability that screen out more of one class of persons than other classes of persons. In itself, disparate effect may not constitute a violation of Title VII, but its existence usually creates that suspicion and indicates that close examination of the screening processes, criteria, or neutrality of application is warranted. An employer may be able to justify the disparate effect of hiring criteria by showing their job-relatedness and the neutrality of their application, but the employer always bears the burden of proof.

distribution rate

(1) The degree (percentages) to which a given protected class is employed in the various job titles, job classes, and other units within the employing organization; and (2) the degree (percentages) to which individuals of a given protected class are involved in various employment transactions (for example, applications for employment, hiring, placement, promotion, separation, etc.).

employment process

Under Title VII, the employment process includes recruitment, applicant flow, hiring, job placement, compensation, promotion, transfer, termination, shift assignments, geographical and departmental assignments, and all other such activities.

external labor area

The geographic area from which an employer may reasonably be expected to recruit new workers. In a compliance sense, this total labor market has submarkets within it, comprised of persons with the requisite skills, experience, etc., to fill given jobs.

external labor market
> The civilian work force within a labor area.

incidence rate
> A measurement of the degree to which a specific protected class is involved in any of the various steps of the employment process. If there are 80 black males of whom 20 are promoted, the incidence rate is 25 percent. As a measure of compliance, the incidence rate is compared with the degree to which the specific protected class is represented in the external labor market.

parity
> In the EEO context, parity is used to describe a condition in which the percentage participation of protected classes in an organization (and/or its units, job classes, etc.) is identical to the equivalent percentages in the external labor area. There are two types of parity:
>
> 1. Population parity, which compares the percentage participation of the protected classes in an organization with their percentage participation in the appropriate external labor force.
>
> 2. Occupational parity, which compares the percentage participation of the protected classes in distinct occupational categories in the organization with the participation of these classes in the same categories in the appropriate external labor force.

participation rate
> (1) The percentage of incumbents of a job title, class, department or other organization unit (including the whole organization) who belong to a given protected class; and (2) the percentage of individuals involved in an employment process transaction (for example, application for employment, hiring, placement, promotion, separation) who belong to a given protected class.

personnel policies and practices
> All rules and operations through which an organization recruits, hires, places, transfers, promotes, and separates employees; administers wages and benefits; and all other terms, conditions, and privileges of employment.

present effects of past patterns of discrimination
> The EEOC and the courts have consistently held that employers are liable for correcting situations in which employees continue to suffer the "present effects of past patterns of discrimination." Simply stated, this can mean that an employee (or group of employees) who should (in the eyes of the Commission and/or the courts) have been promoted three years ago (whether a complaint has been lodged or not) is still entitled to be "made whole." Being made whole can be accomplished through retroactive pay or other costly means.

protected classes

Title VII of the Civil Rights Act of 1964 proscribes discrimination on the basis of race, color, religion, sex, or national origin. The generic term "protected class" (with no precise legal meaning) is used to describe those groups who have borne, in the eyes of Congress and the courts, the brunt of discriminatory employment practices in the past, namely women and minorities. However, all persons, regardless of race, religion, sex, etc., are protected by Title VII in the sense that they may not be denied equal employment opportunity.

relevant labor pool

The total number of incumbent employees who are in position for a specific promotion, or all candidates who could conceivably be considered for a promotion.

systemic discrimination

Equal employment opportunity may be denied through the inevitable consequence of some established business practice, persisting over a period of time, rather than of a specific overt action against an aggrieved party. Such a result of the "system" is systemic discrimination and has been at the root of most Title VII settlements to date. Inadvertent and usually unintentional, the disparate effect produced by systemic discrimination constitutes a prime area of vulnerability for most businesses.

utilization analysis

An audit of the current distribution, participation, compensation, and movements of an organization's employees. The analysis is made by job grade, title, and lines of progression for all sex and race groups, across all units of the organization, for each step of the employment process. Current distribution must be analyzed in terms of relevant external labor markets, and such comparisons must be made at each step of the employment process. A utilization analysis establishes a legal and accurate basis for realistic goal setting.

Selected Readings

"Affirmative Action: Why Isn't It Working?" by Oscar A. Ornati and Anthony F. Pisano. *The Personnel Administrator*, September 1972.

Employment Practices Decisions. Chicago: Commerce Clearing House, Inc. New volumes added periodically.

Employment, Race and Poverty, A. M. Ross and H. Hill, editors. New York: Harcourt Brace, 1967.

Internal Labor Markets and Manpower Analysis, by Peter B. Doeringer and Michael J. Piore. Lexington, Mass.: Heath, 1971.

Non-Discrimination in Employment: "Changing Perspectives 1963–1972." New York: The Conference Board, 1974.

Racial Discrimination in Employment, by M. I. Sovern. New York: The Twentieth Century Fund, 1966.

Spanish Surnamed American Employment in the Southwest, by F. H. Schmidt. Colorado Civil Rights Commission, N.D.

"A Total Approach to EEO Compliance," by Edward J. Giblin and Oscar A. Ornati. *Personnel*, September–October 1974.

The following titles are published by the Equal Employment Opportunity Commission and are available through any of the Commission's regional offices.

Affirmative Action and Equal Employment: A Guidebook for Employers (2 vols.), 1974.

Equal Employment Opportunity and Affirmative Action: A Guidebook for Employers on Voluntary Programs, 1974.

The Foundation of Equal Employment Opportunity, by Alfred W. Blumrosen (2 vols.), 1972.

Guidelines on Employment Testing Procedures, 1970.

The Legislative History of Title VII, 1969.